GOSSIP
BOYS

THE UNAUTHORISED BIOGRAPHY OF
CHACE CRAWFORD

GOSSIP BOYS

THE UNAUTHORISED BIOGRAPHY OF
CHACE CRAWFORD

LIZ KAYE

10 9 8 7 6 5 4 3 2 1

First published in the UK in 2011 by Virgin Books,
an imprint of Ebury Publishing
A Random House Group Company

www.randomhouse.co.uk

Addresses for companies within The Random House Group Limited can be
found at www.randomhouse.co.uk/offices.htm

The Random House Group Limited Reg. No. 954009

A CIP catalogue record for this book is available from the British Library

ISBN: 978075340282

The Random House Group Limited supports The Forest Stewardship
Council (FSC®), the leading international forest certification organisation.
Our books carrying the FSC label are printed on FSC® certified paper. FSC is
the only forest certification scheme endorsed by the leading environmental
organisations, including Greenpeace. Our paper procurement policy can be
found at www.randomhouse.co.uk/environment

Printed and bound by CPI Group (UK) Ltd, Croydon, CR0 4YY
To buy books by your favourite authors and register for offers visit
www.randomhouse.co.uk

Contents

CHAPTER 1

Early Life

SEVENTEEN:

Fill in the blank: When I was 17, I was _____

CHACE CRAWFORD:

'Ignorant. No, I was ... very fortunate. No, I was ...
spunky. I was ... rebellious. Black sheep of the family.
Any one of those. I was ... happy to graduate from high
school. I was ... in Texas. I was ... loving life at 17. It
was easier, less complicated. I was ... simple. How 'bout
that? I was just simple.

THE SIMPLE LIFE IS the very opposite of what Chace
Crawford's character in *Gossip Girl* enjoys. Nate
Archibald lives in the ultra-wealthy Upper East Side of
Manhattan where his world is a whirlwind of parties,
limousines, girls and complicated, turbulent relationships. In
terms of emotional upheaval, Nate's life is almost the exact
opposite of the childhood that Chace Crawford was lucky

enough to experience. Chace was born in Lubbock in the north-western corner of Texas, the birthplace of many prominent country musicians and basketball stars such as Craig Ehlo and Daniel Santiago, as well as football player Mason Crosby. Possibly its most famous resident was the 1950s rock and roll legend Buddy Holly!

However, when Chace was just a young boy, his family relocated 300 miles directly east past Fort Worth to the city of Plano, and so he spent much of his childhood in and around Dallas, a city he loves to this day. Notable Plano residents include legendary cyclist Lance Armstrong and golfer Fred Couples.

Chace was born on 18 July 1985 with a host of famous names: Nelson Mandela, astronaut John Glenn and billionaire entrepreneur Richard Branson. His full name is actually Christopher Chace Crawford, but he chooses to use his more distinctive middle moniker.

The Crawford family was very hard-working and were clearly fortunate to live in Plano – in 2005 the city was voted the 'Best Place to Live' in the western United States. And it's here that such well-known and distinctive American brands Pizza Hut, JC Penney and Dr Pepper are located, so perhaps their presence contributes to the area's affluence. It consistently ranks highly in the list of America's wealthiest cities (being rated the wealthiest in 2008) and in 2010 it won the equally enviable accolade as 'The Safest City to live in America'. Shades of Nate Archibald's own lifestyle perhaps? Chace himself seems acutely aware of his privileged upbringing and openly speaks of his gratitude: 'The best thing about [living in the South],' he told *Female First*, 'is the way I was raised. I'm so thankful for my background. I feel like I've got a good head on my shoulders and that my parents raised me right. I just love the people there in general in the South. It's a great atmosphere and a great place to actually live – so I'm really thankful for that.'

Chace's father Chris is a dermatologist while his mother Dana is a teacher. His parents had met at a young age ('it's a Southern thing!') and by the time his father was at med school, Chace's mum was expecting his younger sister Candice. According to Chace, a huge upside of starting their family this young is that his parents are still young themselves; he felt the full benefit of this when his acting career took off in his late teens and early twenties because his mum and dad encouraged and advised him through the firestorm of international fame and fortune without the distance of a generation gap.

Chace paints a lovely picture of a very close family sitting down to eat his mother's beautiful chicken and rice. 'My mom kept the household together, managed everything. We were her life.' The closeness of the Crawford family has remained even though their son is now a superstar actor – fast forward to 2011 and Chace is a very famous face on the TV, but without fail he still phones his parents every single day.

And yes, Chace's stunning looks were there from a very young age! His sister Candice is also fortunate in the looks department and has gone on to become a beauty queen. Chace himself has spoken about this familial beauty to blockbuster.co.uk: 'I'm blessed. I have a beautiful mother and beautiful father so I guess you could say I'm blessed with good genes.' He says his father never really bombarded him with skincare tips but there would often be family friends' girls in the kitchen where his dad would help them out with their teenage skincare worries. In later years, when Chace had become a famous TV star, he joked with reporters about how much his father's profession affected his looks: 'He would give me face wash, I had Botox age nine, that's when we started. And then just the occasional facelift.'

It wasn't all roses for Chace, however. He attended Ridgeview Elementary and it was here that his mum made him wear 'crazily' brief cut-off jeans. 'I suffered from it. But at least I learned quite early that there's no reason for men to wear shorts.' On a more serious note, when talking to *ES* magazine on a promotional trip to the UK in 2010, Chace shocked his many fans by revealing that he was diagnosed – incorrectly, in his opinion – with Attention Deficit Disorder or ADD. He was even prescribed a drug to alleviate the condition but this was something he would later feel was an overreaction: 'I don't think I am ADD. Now I'm much more interested in knowledge and learning. I watch a lot of documentaries and news, I have a hunger for that. As a kid, I was more interested in daydreaming and friends ... They used to really overprescribe that stuff ... Maybe it was good I took a little bit of medication, y'know? To help facilitate my schoolwork.' He admits that at times he would utilise his 'wild imagination' and draw 'masterpieces of the stupidest things!'

Not surprisingly Chace's good looks attracted a lot of female attention at school! He was relatively shy but very popular and as he grew older his confidence began to grow. His first kiss, at the age of 11, was in sixth grade when his class was on summer camp. All of his mates had girlfriends and he really liked one particular girl. Despite admitting that he was 'a very awkward kisser', he is warmly sentimental about this pre-teenage romance: '[My first kiss] was very picturesque on this cliff with my first girlfriend, Kiley. She was my best friend's twin sister. I'm actually good friends with her today!' When it came to Valentine's Day, Chace gave Kiley a home-made mixtape.

The Crawford family spent four years in Bloomington, Minnesota which is why there are hints of that region's accent in Chace's soft voice, rather than just a pure Texan drawl. From his early teens, Chace attended Trinity Christian Academy whose website states it 'is an independent co-educational school that offers a college preparatory curriculum within a Christian community committed to integrating Biblical faith and learning. The school desires to educate and develop the whole person for the glory of God by helping equip each student to grow in the grace and knowledge of

Jesus Christ, and to become a faithful disciple of Him.' The religious choice of school mirrored the Crawford family's values – Chace was raised as a Southern Baptist and they attended church regularly.

Fees to attend the school (as of 2011) can be as much as $16,000. The campus places a strong emphasis on sports with over fifty teams, including baseball, wrestling and football. Not surprisingly, perhaps, the school also has several fine arts courses such as visual arts, drama and choir.

The school was a relatively small establishment and when he was a star on *Gossip Girl*, Chace would often be asked how his own school days at a private campus compare to the very privileged life that the characters on the hit show enjoy: 'It's just different, I learnt about the bubble [though], a really small high school, that whole situation and the gossip, the smaller it gets the worse it is.'

Chace was a strong sportsman at high school and was said to particularly excel at golf with a handicap of six, which earned him a slot on the college team. In fact, he played so much golf that even the aroma of a neatly clipped green brings him out all sporty: 'When I smell freshly cut grass I get this air of competition,' he told reporter Lisa Ingrassia. 'It wakes me up, gets me going. It energises me in a certain way. It's liberating.' With this golfing background in mind, he once said, 'I was a nerd, quite awkward', yet he was also excellent at the more macho sport of American football, playing as quarterback.

Chace was also a talented artist and after he hit the big time with *Gossip Girl* he filled his bachelor's apartment with numerous stunning works of art and would spend hours going around the various art galleries in Chelsea Pier, New York. Back when he was a teenage boy, he worked primarily with watercolours, charcoal and pastels, though as an adult he tends to concentrate on sketching. It was during this time that he also developed quite a skill for photography, buying a 35mm camera and teaching himself the techniques required. He later credited this skill with helping his acting, as he said the techniques needed to compose a good photograph gave him a deeper understanding of the composition that a director has to achieve on set. 'Everything was so intriguing to me,' he told *Female First*, 'and I really fell in love with [art] you know. Art has now become a part of me, and a part of my life because it's so interesting.'

However, for the teenage Chace, there were also far more serious events around the corner, as he revealed in an interview with *Fabulous* magazine: 'I went to juvenile detention when I was 15. It was all over a little misunderstanding with a pellet gun! I accidentally hit somebody on a golf course so I went to the centre for the weekend. At the time my parents went ballistic, but it's a joke now.'

Looking back on those (relatively!) innocent days, Chace describes himself as quite a shy teenager prone to over-analysing situations, 'a bit over-zealous', as he puts it. Still, the usual teenage rites of passage seem to have been something he enjoyed: when he was 16 his father gave him a black Chevy

Tahoe truck in which he would 'basically drive around and wreck things'. Girls went hand in hand with his wheels. 'So much happened in it,' he later cheekily told *People* magazine, 'I can't even tell you how emotional it was to get rid of that truck!'

Chace has also detailed an 'awkward' phase in high school when he felt very much less than the local hunk – he had braces on his teeth for a year and then followed that up by having blond tips in his hair. 'That was my absolute low point,' he later laughed. Yet he was eventually voted 'Best Dressed' in his senior year of high school.

He says he wasn't bullied at school although there was a tradition that when every pupil reached the age of 16, they had to be beaten up by their 'mates' 16 times! 'You just had to take it. It did hurt – I didn't get cut, but I got some pretty good welts.'

One of his summer jobs at high school was working at Abercrombie & Fitch – which he hated! 'They play the same three CDs all day long. They play it so loud you can't even talk in the store and they blast the place with cologne, you can smell it from a block away. I was a greeter. I had to stand out front and time would drag on. I'd beg them to let me work on the cash register.' Interestingly, this job led to modelling work for their sibling store, Hollister, which aims their products at younger teens.

Chace's stunning good looks meant that his popularity with the girls in junior high continued with the girls at high school.

One of his first girlfriends was unfortunate enough to receive the worst brush-off that Chace would admit to – when he decided he wanted to split up, he left a note under her windscreen wiper! 'I felt like I could get everything out that way. I was only 14. I'll never do that again!' When he was older, he was talked into a blind date but it was a disaster and he swore never to do this again.

Overall, Chace has great memories of his time at Trinity, as he told the *Inquirer*: 'I actually had a great high school experience. My school was small so I got to know everybody.' Towards the end of his time there, two developments arose that would have a massive impact on Chace's future TV career. It was while he was in his senior year that Chace had his very first experience of acting. Before this, he'd often quoted famous movie lines around the house but only as a boyish bit of fun with no thoughts about a career. However, while at Trinity his drama teacher asked him if he would audition for a role in a production of *The Boyfriend*. Chace duly did – choosing to sing the National Anthem – and he won the part. At this stage, however, even winning this sought-after role did not incite in Chace a burning passion for the stage: 'It was a good little role and something about it was just fun, but it didn't even really trigger anything in me.' Qualifying this indifference a little more, he explained that he hadn't enjoyed the singing part of the musical (by his own admission he is 'not the best singer in the world'), but the acting side had interested him and it was probably this debut production that started the flicker of interest that would eventually lead him to *Gossip Girl*.

Also while attending Trinity (from where he graduated in 2003), Chace had begun some low-key modelling work, principally around Dallas – he later said he 'hated' this line of work as it didn't always pay too well and they treated the models 'like a piece of meat'. Some of these modelling snaps later appeared on the Internet after he had broken big in *Gossip Girl* and show him without a shirt and wearing a cowboy's tasselled leather jacket and ten-gallon hat, in a stereotypical 'beefcake' pose. His famous eyebrows were already very prominent, a feature later described as 'the greatest eyebrows this side of Zac Efron'. Chace himself has been less complimentary, saying, 'They're like Brillo pads! But I just kinda let 'em go. I don't like looking that clean.'

It was during his mid-to-late teens that Chace began a relationship that to this day is his longest with any girl, over three years. Somehow – in true Nate Archibald style! – he 'ended up dating one of her friends!' After this drama, Chace chose to stay resolutely single for some time to come, no wonder!

CHAPTER 2

Decision Time

AFTER HIS EVENTFUL HIGH school years, it was off to Malibu's Pepperdine University, an enviable place to study, situated as it is on an 830-acre campus overlooking the Pacific Ocean. As with Trinity, there was an emphasis on religion with the small Jesuit university proudly saying: 'It is the purpose of Pepperdine University to pursue the very highest academic standards within a context that celebrates and extends the spiritual and ethical ideals of the Christian faith.'

It is widely reported that Chace was a member of the Sigma Nu fraternity at Pepperdine, although their official website has no mention of him under their 'Famous Members' section (Harrison Ford was a member though!). Notable other entertainment alumni from Pepperdine include former Miss World, Lisa-Marie Kohrs, R&B star Montell Jordan, and George Schlatter, the Emmy-winning American television producer and director, best known for *Rowan and Martin's Laugh-In.*

It was at Pepperdine in his fraternity house that Chace had his first 'supernatural' experience when he saw a strange, ethereal figure that soon vanished. This left him with the view that ghosts and spirits definitely exist – a belief that in the future would prove to be remarkably appropriate for one of his first cinematic roles.

In another nod to his future role in *Gossip Girl*, many of the fellow pupils at Pepperdine were from very wealthy families: 'There were a lot of kids there whose families were very rich. The parents would be on private jets on business trips all the time and, although you could see they loved their kids, they weren't there.' Chace's course at Pepperdine was journalism, but he would switch majors twice because he was unsure of his career ambitions. Famous faces often admit they had no idea of an exact career path at first, but *always* knew they didn't want to conform; Chace is no exception: 'I never felt I would have a desk job,' he told *VMan*. 'I knew I had to fulfil my creative side, my creative needs.'

Consequently Chace kept chopping and changing his degree, with journalism, advertising, business and communication majors all being studied. 'Everyone else knew what they wanted to do. But not me – I was the lone wolf,' he once told *Teen Vogue*. With great honesty, he has since admitted to feeling genuinely 'confused' during this phase of his university studies and that he often worried about how his peer group all seemed to know what they wanted to do (he has since realised that this perception was 'complete bullshit'). One of the few activities that Chace definitely enjoyed – alongside more golf, football and other sports – was acting, which he had started doing at university as a hobby but became increasingly captivated by as the terms went by. Over time he realised that acting was where his passion actually lay; maybe, just maybe it could also be where his career was destined to take him?

With this exciting realisation, Chace became suddenly very focused indeed on his future. He started going to acting lessons most evenings and he was beginning to adore the idea of working in the profession. During this time, a friend suggested he contact a TV commercials agent. Hollywood legend has it that when the completely stunning Chace Crawford took his friend's advice and walked into the agent's office, the admirably visionary agent took one look at him and said, 'Welcome … Yes!'

A handful of adverts followed but Chace was always looking for serious acting opportunities. Perhaps not surprisingly, given his recent modelling work and incredible good looks, it wasn't long before Chace secured himself an acting agent too. The very first agent who interviewed him snapped him up and put Chace straight on his books. In his initial interview, it's rumoured that the agent asked him, 'Can you do improv?' to which the green-behind-the-ears Chace responded, 'What's improv?'

Once signed to the acting agent, Chace began studying theatrical techniques even more intensely and his fierce ambition and hard work soon reaped dividends. He found that the majority of acting class students weren't really focused and didn't apply themselves. By contrast, he felt there was no point being there at all unless he committed himself 100 per cent.

After just a year of his broadcast journalism major, his acting career looked like it was starting to take off. 'I was just only sure of what I didn't want to do,' he told Josh Clinton of *Prime Time Pulse*: 'I was young, I had a year ahead of everyone else in school … a friend of a friend put me through to [that] commercial agent and they agreed to work with me. That got the ball rolling for me, and [later] it all started to click for me in acting class.' He's also modestly said he 'sort of fell into a little acting during that time'. What is clear is that he was very driven – now he had found a career that he was passionate about, he was going to aim high and work hard. Signing to the agents was a brilliant start: 'Finding someone who will push you and believe in you, that's the first big step,' he later told *Wonderland* magazine, 'and I started getting really good feedback right away.'

He still wasn't convinced though; commuting between college and various short-notice auditions was proving to be practically very difficult and when his father asked him how things were going one day, Chace was totally honest. 'Listen, I'm half-assing both things, Dad,' he admitted. To his amazement, his dad told him to take some time out of school and go full-on for the acting life.

Encouraged in this fantastic way, Chace decided to take a semester off, principally to see if a sharper focus on acting might reap results. Rather than chide him for wasting his education, his very supportive parents were totally behind their son: 'It was a practical move,' his mother has since said, explaining that Chace had taken a career aptitude test that suggested he was best suited for a job in the performing arts. In later interviews Chace regularly references this aptitude test, so it must have had quite an effect on him.

However, like millions of aspiring actors before him, Chace had no income so he would make ends meet by working as a car valet, grinding out a meagre living parking vehicles at a seaside restaurant in Malibu. He's admitted to sometimes stealing his customer's chewing gum from their glove compartments and even declared that he wasn't even that good at the job anyway! One day the famous and notorious rap music mogul Suge Knight came in and Chace was so nervous that he asked a colleague to move Suge's car! Years later, when Chace was a hot Hollywood property, Wrigley's chewing gum heard the story of the illicit chewing-gum raids on customers' cars and sent him a load of free gum, saying that he didn't have to steal it from glove boxes any more!

Despite the very modest pay, Chace really enjoyed his time as a valet and later called it 'one of the best jobs I've ever had. I loved it.' The site was next to the beach and as a petrol-head he thoroughly enjoyed being around swanky cars all day. However, acting was his bug and he knew that valeting cars was only ever a way of putting food on the table. Luckily, Chace's first ever movie role was just around the corner …

Like all aspiring actors, Chace was not in a position to pick and choose his roles as he would be able to in his post-*Gossip Girl* years. Although many fans think his first screen time came with the 2006 film, *Covenant* (more of which later), in fact his debut was some five months earlier, in a made-for-television film called *Long Lost Son*, originally broadcast in the summer of 2006.

The project was directed by Brian Trenchard-Smith, an English producer, director and actor who had made a name for himself with many films in the horror and action genres in Australia. His most notable successes were films such as *The Man from Hong Kong* and the award-winning *The Quest*.

The film was made by Lifetime Television, an American network that focuses on movies, sitcoms and dramas aimed at the female viewer, most often with a woman in the lead role (until 2005, the channel's tag line was 'Television for Women'). Comedians have been known to refer to Lifetime as 'The Estrogen Channel' or 'Wifetime'. So it's perhaps not entirely surprising that it was on just such a channel that the astoundingly handsome Chace Crawford got his first break!

Long Lost Son opens with Kristen, a doting young mother, played by Gabrielle Anwar (perhaps best known for her tango with Al Pacino in *Scent of a Woman*) lying next to her young son on the floor, painting, chatting and laughing together. Their joy is interrupted by the arrival of her estranged husband; their troubled marriage is heading for a divorce and while living apart the son starts to see his father only once a month at weekends. On one visit, despite asking her ex not to take their son out sailing as a dangerous storm is approaching, he does exactly that, which leads to the apparent disaster that underpins the entire movie.

Father and son head out on their boat the *Ocean Dreamer* in a foul storm; not long after they set off however, a radio signal reports they are having difficulties and have lost a mast. Soon after that, the ship is reported 'Lost at Sea' with no sign of any survivors.

Retreating into a shell of grief and despair, Kristen slowly rebuilds her life and eventually remarries. However, while unwittingly watching a friend's holiday video 14 years after the disaster, Kristen sees a man in the footage she knows to be her apparently 'dead' ex-husband, who is running a diving school for tourists on the island of Santa Alicia, evidently under an alias.

That is shocking enough, but then it becomes apparent that the young man working next to her ex-husband in the video footage is the long lost son of the film's title. Chace has to wait until nearly twenty minutes into the film to make his appearance in this holiday video footage and even then it is only for a few seconds; appropriately perhaps given his latterday sex symbol status, he does so with his shirt off and wearing only a pair of shorts, preparing the tourist boat for a four-day cruise. As he chats to the hand-held video camera, Kristen realises that he is in fact her son; she rewinds the tape and freezes the picture on her ex-husband. That's when it dawns on her – they are both still alive. Kristen later discovers that the 'fatal' boat accident was in fact faked and that both her husband and 18-year-old son are alive and living on a Caribbean island. The entire ruse was in order for the husband to gain full custody of the son.

She discovers the exact location of the two men and learns from locals that her son is very popular. 'He's shaping up to be a real heartbreaker with the holiday girls that come in during the season,' one local tells her, which all Chace fans would certainly agree with! She eventually tracks down their boat and Chace reappears, this time in even fewer clothes, snorkelling around the harbour.

The handsome young man chats with Kristen and makes her feel very welcome, oblivious to their true relationship. He tells her he is Canadian and to her shock recounts how his mother died in a fire when he was only three years old. He later waxes lyrical about the travels he has been on with his father and proudly tells how his dad makes businesses and sells them on before relocating again.

From a technical point of view, Chace's dialogue seems very natural and fluid and does not fall victim to the stunted and wooden acting that so many made-for-TV films suffer from. From hereon in, it is he and Gabrielle who are the stars of the movie and the obvious highlights of the film. When Chace's character tells Kristen about his 'dead' mother, there is a genuine sense of dramatic tension that belies the humble made-for-TV backdrop.

Kristen admires her son from a distance – although for different reasons to most of the audience! – and when her ex-husband is caught trying to abscond again, he admits to Chace about who she actually is. Once mother and son are reunited, the realisation of what has happened leads to many troubling questions. Sadly, in gaining a mother, Chace's character loses his father, as his dad sails off into a storm and is later marooned on a desert island. Meanwhile, Chace's character and his mum head back to LA to start a new life.

It's a sign of Chace's latterday fame that despite the heart-wrenching plot and the emotionally laden storyline, most of the comments online about the movie centre around his looks, perhaps the favourite being, 'OMG, Chace is a hawtiee!' Although Chace's character didn't have the majority of dialogue, with the focus mostly on Gabrielle, he made sufficient impact to turn heads both for his looks and acting abilities.

Speaking to Christopher Bollen of *Interview Magazine*, however, Chace was rather awkward when asked about this early foray into acting. 'At that point I'm obviously taking anything I could get. I'm thinking, *Oh god. How do I even, like, craft this into something believable?* The woman they cast as my mom was like, 36 and smoking hot. She still is!' Chace became good friends with Gabrielle Anwar on set and has remained so ever since.

Her beauty and youthful looks caused Chace to worry about the credibility of his character's authenticity, namely with such a 'hot' mother being so young: 'This is going to look like I'm attracted to her – like when she finds me, I'm not supposed to know she's my mom, you know?' There were other equally obvious question marks surrounding the movie: when the 'reveal' exposes Chace as the long lost son of the film's title, the ex-husband and wife get on with surprisingly civility after a philosophical 'He's a good kid' platitude from a mother who has spent 14 years of torture grieving for a boy she has now discovered is alive. After his father heads off into the darkened stormy skies, Chace's character is next seen chatting merrily with his 'new' mother, heading off to LA seemingly without a care in the world, with no apparent sense of confusion, anger or bewilderment. It feels like an emotional loose end.

Critics are usually very snooty about so-called 'made-for-TV' films such as this; often the plots are derided, formulaic and very weak and the cast are usually mostly first-timers or those struggling for success. The satirical cartoon series *Family Guy* once spoofed the channel as 'Television for Idiots', including the movie *Men are Terrible and Will Hurt You Because This Is Lifetime*.

However, the flipside of this rather negative view is that such projects are also a priceless proving ground for many actors and there is a very long list of massive film and TV stars who have started off in this genre. Likewise, the directors behind such projects are often harshly scoffed for similar reasons; yet Brian Trenchard-Smith who headed up *Long Lost Son* is in fact cited by none other than Quentin Tarantino as one of the *Pulp Fiction* mastermind's favourite directors. The quirky sense of humour and large scale of Trenchard-Smith's work even led to an award-winning documentary about his early career called *Not Quite Hollywood*. The director also had a knack for discovering new talent, having premiered a 15-year-old Nicole Kidman in 1983's *BMX Bandits*. Similarly, when he worked with Chace, it was obvious to the director that here was a new star with great potential: 'I knew from his first scene, he was going to be hot,' Trenchard-Smith would later say.

Critics seemed to agree; Gabrielle Anwar was widely praised for her part but so Chace was too. Take this quote from Andrew L Urban on UrbanCineFile.com: 'It's Gabrielle Anwar's performance ... that makes the film so engaging [and] her 18-year-old son [is] played effortlessly by the handsome and likeable Chace Crawford.' Other reviews were less flattering about the film but indirectly hailed Chace, such as this quote from the rather fantastic and funny www.mothermayisleepwithlifetime.blogspot.com: 'If you insist on watching this movie, fast forward to about the middle, once a hot teenage kid with his shirt off appears.'

It is simply not true that Chace's screen debut made him an overnight star; in fact, most fans were not even aware of this opening performance until long after he had made it big in *Gossip Girl*. However, what *Long Lost Son* did achieve was a solid start for Chace's acting career – as one of the stand-out actors in the film, he had made his first mark.

CHAPTER 3

Warlocks and Worries

'There have been a few girls that have gotten away that
I wish I could put a spell on – make them fall in love
with me.'

Chace Crawford speaking at the time of his first cinematic
movie release, words he would probably never have to use
again.

ALTHOUGH *LONG LOST SON* was his first actual aired
screen appearance, that made-for-TV movie wasn't
actually the first professional acting work he'd experienced. In
2004, while still at Pepperdine, he had begun filming a
supernatural thriller called *Covenant*. This was a film intended
for cinematic release, and as such Chace's first mainstream
movie role. Filming began in Canada in 2004 but the actual

movie's release was not until December 2006 by which time *Long Lost Son* had earned the right to be called Chace's first on-screen outing.

How Chace came to win the role in this new movie is typical of his ambition: he had sent a videotape of himself to the producers and received a request to be met in person, a 'call back'. That call back had led to auditions and Chace was exhilarated to win the role of Tyler, a 16-year-old warlock.

Directed by Renny Harlin, who was at the helm of *Cliffhanger*, as well as movies from the *Die Hard* franchise, and written by J S Cardone, *Covenant* recounts the tale of five seventeenth-century families from the Ipswich Colony of Massachusetts, who were supernaturally possessed with 'The Power' and formed a vow of silence in order to avoid being killed by the witch-hunting gangs that were prowling the new territory in those dark years. However, one family was a rogue spirit and was banished from the Covenant, mysteriously disappearing without a trace for centuries, only to turn up in modern-day America. (It is a common misconception that *Covenant* was based around a cartoon or graphic novel but this is not the case. There is a comic book of the same name, but this is unrelated to Chace's movie debut. Matters were made more complicated by the fact that a graphic novel of the movie was also later made.)

Descendants of these original five families have since settled in the town of Spencer and it is their intertwining lives that the film is focused around. As teenage warlocks, the sons of that seventeenth-century coven of witches have all been born with supernatural powers such as invincibility, shape-shifting, flight and super-strength. But each time the four 'Sons of Ipswich' use some of their addictive powers, they age prematurely, disastrously eroding their own life expectancy ... and they soon start to be hunted and haunted by so-called 'darklings', undead visions bent on destroying them.

These four teenage men are the central characters of the film; Chace plays Tyler Simms, the youngest of the foursome, and it is a sign of his still fledgling career that in the opening credits his name is only the sixth to flash up on-screen. Talking about his character in a promo interview for the film, Chace described him thus: '[Tyler's] kind of the youngest one. He's a junior in high school and he looks up to the other boys. He's kinda the rookie guy that just wants to use the power and be along for the joyride. It's a fun character, just kind of happy go lucky.'

The movie begins when a student is found dead of an apparent 'overdose' following an illicit beach party; thereafter dark secrets begin to unfold. It is the return of the 'long lost' fifth family's son that ramps up the horror. Confusingly, the 'long lost son' this time is also called Chace, albeit his character rather than the actor! This child was orphaned of his adoptive parents in a car accident aged only two, and it is revealed that this kid is the malevolent and vengeful fifth 'son' returning to wreak havoc on the other four warlocks. A climactic battle ensues between the lead Caleb and the evil

Chace, with our Mr Crawford nowhere to be seen. Good conquers evil … but as with many horror movie endings, evil might come back. If a sequel gets commissioned.

The Sony Screen Gems film is a very much more polished and bigger budget affair than *Long Lost Son*. As *People* magazine put it, the film is 'one of those scary movies with pretty people'. As well as the notable young cast, there is a credible soundtrack which includes the likes of White Zombie and Killing Joke.

Chace himself modestly called his contribution merely 'a peripheral role'. It's true that his character is probably the most understated of the four 'Sons'; Steven Strait takes the lead role as Caleb opposite Laura Ramsey playing Sarah. And there are lengthy sections of the film when Chace makes no appearance whatsoever. His six-pack makes a showing in the swimming pool and shower scene while a subsequent swimming race ups the 'hunk' quota with rather obvious lashings of torso. When Chace does appear, he looks strikingly young, easily accommodating his character's sixteen years. In a jovial nod to his character's deference to others, when asked what his favourite scene was, he said, 'There's a group scene where we're all at Nicky's Bar [but] … any close-up on me, that's my favourite!'

The film utilises many of the horror clichés, such as dark, spooky buildings, thunderstorms, cavernous crypts filled with candles (surely it must takes ages to light them all?), mysterious figures hiding in shadows and an ending that blatantly leaves open the opportunity for a sequel when the key 'bad guy' is nowhere to be found. In fact, some observers might suggest there were more stereotypes on offer here than in Chace's more 'unfashionable' made-for-TV debut film.

The plot is fairly slow-moving as indeed is the dialogue at times, and although the sense of suspense does ramp up as the film's climax approaches, there were some critics who felt the film was padded out, overweight and dwelled too obviously on the four male hunks in the lead roles. Not that any Chace Crawford fans were complaining about that! When Chace does have dialogue, it's fair to say there's a certain intensity that later fans of *Gossip Girl* would recognise.

It was quite a physical film for Chace too, with the four lead males often being thrown through the air, flying over the heads of other cast members or being smashed into walls and windows in violent fights. Chace's already toned physique was put through the mill as there were at least two swimming sessions per day to meet the target of twelve hours a week training in the pool that the producers desired – mindful of the inevitable emphasis on the boys' looks but also so that the crucial 'swimming pool' scene in the movie looked legitimate.

Further, before filming began Chace was required to train for weeks on so-called 'wire work', where an actor is strapped to a heavyweight safety wire, which will later be used for filming a 'flying' sequence. To make any such flying action look realistic takes a great deal of skill and also considerable physical prowess, but Chace relished the challenge: 'We did a lot of wire work and spent a lot of time at the gym. That was probably one of the most fun aspects of the whole shoot actually – getting to go and practise on this really cool wire rigging computerised motion kind of set. It was really fun to get on there and go to town on it – it was just great.' Cheekily, he added, 'There were no real-life warlocks though. It was definitely all stunts and what not!' He has also said that he likes to do 'all his own stunts' wherever possible as he feels this make the footage look more authentic and 'real'.

One example of his eagerness to inject all his scenes with authenticity actually came with the very first shot of the movie. The four teenage warlocks are shown walking to a cliff's edge, looking down at a beach party under way. Then, without warning, they simply walk off the edge, but instead of plummeting to their deaths, they gently float to the sandy ground below. Like much of the film, this effect was created against a green screen and this was Chace's first experience of this technology, which inevitably makes new demands on any actor: 'We were just stood still in the middle of a studio with some green screen around us at 9 a.m. So we had to deal with that – being completely stationary and acting like we're falling off the edge of a cliff.' Chace's fall was particularly difficult as his character dropped off backwards! Funnily, the one 'stunt' he says he would not undertake is any scene with spiders which in real life he doesn't like at all!

The supernatural backdrop to the film meant that many of the sequences were shot at night and in fact the whole of the first month was filmed during night-time, with five days on and Monday/Tuesday off. These night shifts were particularly tiring and in their downtime most of the cast just slept. Another challenge was the bitterly cold weather in Canada, which for Chace – a resident of Malibu – came as quite a shock! At one point when filming near a lake, the water had completely frozen solid. He got in the habit of taking very hot showers between takes just to stay warm. Asked if the cast found other ways to 'keep warm', Chace's fellow cast member Toby replied with a wry smile: 'We don't drink! What is sex? No, we got along really well, guys and girls, from day one. There are no assholes around. We've been out around Montreal, it's a great town!'

As it was Chace's first experience of a cinematic movie, he was understandably curious to see how the director Renny operated, but he was quickly put at ease; indeed, the director and cast got along famously and would even socialise in the (very few!) days off from shooting. Chace is on record as saying that Renny's style was to let the actors enjoy some creative expression with their characters in order to get the best out of them and Crawford really enjoyed this liberal approach.

It wasn't just the director that Chace had to impress though – none other than the president and vice-president of Sony Entertainment were frequently on set, adding to the pressure on the young actor. Both executives were very proactive in their opinions and would take the cast out for dinner on more than one occasion to discuss certain scenes but also just to relax. Chace wasn't the only inexperienced actor on set – with the exception of Steve Strait, most of the cast were relative newcomers.

Any fears that *Covenant* might be a commercial flop were dismissed brilliantly when it debuted at Number 1 in the film charts, taking $9 million in its first weekend, eventually grossing more than $23 million. That said, the box office success was in stark comparison to the media reception – the movie was widely panned, with critics arguing it was a poor man's *Lost Boys* (a cult classic horror movie from the 1980s that had openly been cited as an influence by the film company and was also a movie that Chace himself said was one of his all-time favourites) and an inferior relative of many horror films and action movies such as *Matrix*. Equally negative comparisons were made to the huge smash show *Buffy The Vampire Slayer*. The influential Rotten Tomatoes website even placed it at Number 31 in its list of the decade's 'Worst of the Worst'. Other media sources pointed to the fact it had been a quiet weekend for new movies and thus hitting Number 1 was somehow less of an achievement.

The critics' pens were sharpened with such quotes as this from *Time Out*: 'Flying scenes, frat-boy face-offs and pyrotechnic punch-ups are punctuated by excruciating expository dialogue, while a nasty whiff of homophobia sits uneasily with the many lingering shots of naked male torsos.' The *Boston Phoenix* said simply it was 'an unbewitching brew of clichés,' while the *Daily Mirror* said, '*Covenant* looks less like a movie and more like an extended boy-band video – and with about the same amount of depth.'

It was comments such as this last remark that threatened to damage Chace's fledgling career most seriously. With striking looks such as his, it is all too easy to be stereotyped into 'hunk' roles and struggle forever after to be taken seriously. 'Himbo' is the unkind phrase that settles on such actors. It was his first taste of the movies, and also his first taste of a critic's panning. The question was: did Chace have what it took to break out of this mould?

In a style that would soon become typical of his positive attitude, Chace could only see benefits from having acted in *Covenant*. Speaking with *Female First* magazine, he made no secret of the fact he felt he was lucky to have landed the role: 'Actually it has taken some getting used to. It was a very surreal experience for me to be honest. It was crazy because it was like my first real job, so to be in a big studio feature film I'm very fortunate in a big way.' He had also received a considerable amount of fan mail and was keen to show his gratitude: 'The people who liked [*Covenant*] really liked it – it's good to have those fans.'

An interesting by-product of filming *Covenant* was that it gave Chace a taste for studying again, albeit acting rather than the journalism he had started to major in back at Pepperdine. Some of the cast of the film had academic backgrounds in acting, such as Toby Hemingway who had a BA in theatre, and Chace respected and was drawn to this more technical approach. Chace also went to see co-star Sebastian Strait during a role on Broadway and this gave the future *Gossip Girl* actor a taste for acting on the stage that he retains to this day.

It was after the release of *Covenant* that Chase was asked to sign his first autograph. He has since admitted that this was a strange feeling – his modesty told him it was 'surreal' and even 'useless' but at the same time he was delighted and not about to take this newfound celebrity for granted. Even his dad phoned and asked him if he could send some signed photos to give out to a few friends!

CHAPTER 4

Gossip Girl

'[I'm also working on] *Gossip Girl* – a pilot of a TV
show that I just shot in New York last month. It's
based on a book series – a very popular series, mainly
with the girls here in America. It's based on this
group of teenagers from an elite private school in
New York. They're the popular kids in Manhattan ...
It's got a good chance of being picked up and a good
shot of being a real hit series in the fall, so keep an
eye out ... '

Chace Crawford speaking to *Female First* magazine in early
2007, before the launch of *Gossip Girl*.

2007 WAS THE YEAR that Chace Crawford exploded on to
the scene. He began the year as an aspiring young actor
with a low-key made-for-TV movie on his CV as well as a
Number 1 film that had been critically panned. He would end

2007 as one of the hottest new actors on the planet … how did this happen? Two words: *Gossip Girl*.

The major US TV networks receive hundreds of pitches for new shows each season. Once the elimination process has whittled the numbers down, about 20 will be roughly made into a pilot to test audience interest; roughly a quarter will actually turn into TV shows. In this tough business not all of these survive beyond the first season.

When it was announced that the same team behind *The OC* (the hit teen drama set in Orange Country, California) were creating a new show, there was always going to be huge interest from actors and their agents. Chace was given the script for the pilot of *Gossip Girl* in January 2007 by his new agent; he was very aware of Josh Schwartz's reputation because of *The OC* and so although at first look he felt it was 'typical teen stuff', he also knew it would be very high quality. Chace admits that he wasn't a huge fan of that show; he liked it and watched it, but he wasn't an obsessive. 'I did watch *The OC* a little bit, though,' he told Josh Clinton. 'Back when I was a freshman in college, that was the show to watch. We had our Wednesday night viewing parties and stuff. There was always some great melodrama going on in that show.' The scale of the success of the new TV show would soon take him by surprise: 'Little did I know how insanely popular this series of books were with younger gals … '

Chace was referring to the fact that the new show was based on the bestselling novels by Cecily von Ziegesar, which have sold millions of copies around the world. The books centred around the lives and love interests of a group of girls from Constance Billboard School for Girls, a private elite school in New York's Upper East Side. Originally published in 2002, the books ran to eleven novels, with a prequel and the sequel issued too, proof positive that there was a rich vein of material for any TV show to mine. As with the forthcoming TV series, the content of the novels – at times explicit and often risky – was criticised heavily in some quarters for being inappropriate for a teenage readership. American writer Naomi Wolf called the books 'corruption with a cute overlay'. Notably, the eventual TV series would have some substantial differences to the book series, but these changes made no difference to either project's runaway success.

Back at the auditions for the TV show of the same name, if Chace thought he was a shoe-in, he was in for a shock. Shows like *The OC* don't just get made off the cuff, and Schwartz and his crew are very well known for being absolutely meticulous in their preparation and groundwork. And so the casting process for *Gossip Girl* would prove to be no exception: Chace himself was a hit with the producers from day one in auditions but even so, he was called back six times. Some of these auditions are online and Chace looks extremely young; his acting is adept, despite being in an empty audition room, and on occasion he has to act back to staffers from the production team rather than fellow actors.

Chace had only been acting seriously for three years so as yet he didn't have a formal showreel; he also felt 'pretty new to all of this … it was a learning process'. Nonetheless, he took to the auditions like a natural and kept being called back. His energy was kept high by the appeal of the character he was auditioning for, a rich kid called Nate Archibald: '[On] the first read I thought Nate was totally attainable for me and something I was interested in,' he told Josh Clinton of *Prime Time Pulse*. 'I went in prepared and met with Josh and Stephanie, the director, and casting director, and I guess they liked me. I went in again and again to audition.'

Perhaps not surprisingly given the show's creative team, competition for the lead roles was intense. Although Chace had a couple of movies under his belt, he was relatively inexperienced compared to many of the handsome actors walking in to auditions. Yet his agent was convinced that Chace was the man for the job: 'I think I hit six [auditions],' he told thestar.com, 'The producers were always nice to me and kept calling me back. So I knew I had a chance.'

On his final reading, Chace was paired up with fellow Texan native Leighton Meester who had already been officially cast as Blair Waldorf. 'Leighton was fantastic when I got to read with her,' he later told *MediaBlvd*. 'When I met her and the rest of the cast, I knew it could be something good.'

The final decision over who would get the part of Nate Archibald was left to former actor-turned-CBS president Les

Moonves and Chace got the call to star in the pilot! This did not mean that he was home and dry however. Many pilots are made each year and only a few get to be commissioned and launched as a series – as little as 25 per cent. Pilots often have different actors or actresses in them compared to the final series, so even getting this far was no guarantee of Chace's success. Even if he secured the role of Nate, there was also no guarantee as very often entire characters get written out. Chace's career was still on a knife-edge.

His inexperience was something which he knew stacked the odds again him yet at the same time he seemed to rise to this challenge. Speaking to *MediaBlvd* magazine, he said, 'I've felt like an outsider for the last three years in this business. All the names get the jobs. It's such a political thing. When it gets down to the finals, there's five guys and the producers lay out the resumés. I was always fighting that. I think you have to get over that and start the snowball towards you.'

Despite his admitted relative inexperience, Chace was fully aware of the precarious nature of pilots and the TV commissioning process. He'd already worked two previous pilot seasons, but was undeterred – those who have worked with him all comment on the burning ambition and desire to act that is at the core of his personality. So, when it came to his third so-called 'pilot season', he worked incredibly hard to impress as many executives as possible. As well as the *Gossip Girl* pilot, he also got 'test deal' for a show called *Gravity* – also on CW – which never materialised and a show for MBC too, called *Zip*. So conversely, *Gossip Girl* was by no means assured of capturing Chace's services. With this in mind, Chace sat down with Josh Schwartz and discussed the process and how he was being received; he was told that he was very much one of the front-runners and so along with his agent he decided to focus on *Gossip Girl*. 'It was a good gamble!' he later noted.

His character is Nate Archibald, a stunningly handsome and amenable kid from a very wealthy family who was so alluring that he would sleep with the show's two lead females in the very first episode! As with the source material, Nate was the central character, perhaps even more so in the novels. In the novels he is a lacrosse player at the prestigious St Jude's School for Boys, the son of a French socialite and a wealthy banker. In the TV show his father is described as a wealthy businessman but he does attend the same private school.

Viewers often class the pilot of a series as the 'first' episode and avid fans pride themselves on knowing all about the pilot and how it differs from the eventual series run. Chace was clever with his own personal videotape of the pilot – he showed it to a number of 'real' *Gossip Girl* kids, young adults who actually live the life that the show mimics. He let them watch the pilot and then asked if it was remotely authentic and the answer was a very positive yes!

The link to shows like *The OC* was clear. The complicated love lives of the rich elite in California's Orange County was mirrored in *Gossip Girl* by the equally complex relationships of ultra-wealthy socialites in Upper Manhattan. The platinum credit cards with unlimited spending ceilings, exclusive restaurants and colossal apartments really are the life of this social elite. To give this some context, to buy a one-bed apartment in one of Upper Manhattan's more prestigious blocks would set you back at least $1.5 million; you want to buy a large five-bedroom penthouse? Best set aside at least $10 million. A big townhouse? Think $30–40 million. Each square foot – that's twelve inches by twelve inches of carpet – will cost you at least $1,500 minimum.

The Upper East Side of Manhattan is situated between Central Park and the East River, bordered by 59th Street and 96th Street, as well as the river and Fifth Avenue on Central Park. It is the single most prestigious area to live in the Big Apple, not least by virtue of the cost of homes, and is one of the most exclusive city neighbourhoods in the entire world. The Upper East Side is reputed to contain the greatest concentration of wealth on earth.

This being the case, it attracts very successful people from all walks of life and these are sometimes the sort of folk who will win at all costs. The ability to have anything in life at a price can also sometimes – though not always of course – erode a person's sense of reality and it is this rarefied atmosphere of ultra-wealth that we see has corrupted quite a few of the faces and characters who appear in *Gossip Girl*.

This dynamic has of course been used by Hollywood many times before: among the films which feature the Upper East Side are classics such as *Breakfast At Tiffany's*, *Live and Let Die*, *The Bonfire of the Vanities*, *Eyes Wide Shut* and *American Psycho*. TV is often drawn to the exclusive zip codes of this area too, with shows such as *Friends*, *Diff'rent Strokes*, *Sex and the City* and *Ugly Betty* all being filmed there. Inevitably the area attracts many famous and highly successful residents in real life too, with notable residents including Lady Ga Ga, Sarah Michelle Gellar and Madonna, who paid $40 million for her house there in 2009.

This is the lavish surrounding for *Gossip Girl*'s pilot episode. Opening with 'It Girl' Serena on a train into Manhattan, the pilot episode sees Serena return to the glamorous Upper East Side social circles that *Gossip Girl* chronicles. It isn't long before we are at a glitzy NY party with waiters, rich guests and pearls the size of tennis balls. The narrator of the show is the anonymous blogger Gossip Girl who sends texts and blogs about the friendships and relationships within a group of New York socialites, including Serena van der Woodsen (Blake Lively) and Blair Waldorf (Leighton Meester) as the two centres of attention, then also the boys and girls in their circles such as Dan (Penn Badgley), Nate (Chace), Jenny (Taylor Momsen), Chuck (Ed Westwick), Vanessa (Jessica Szohr), Lily (Kelly Rutherford) and Rufus (Matthew Settle).

Chace's first appearance on-screen is at this party, dressed in a smart suit and blue tie, talking to his overbearing father and his friends about his next educational step (his fashion sense in the pilot is sophisticated, mainly formal suits and less-than-casual wear). Immediately it is obvious that there is a tension between what Nate wants and what his father thinks is best. Then his girlfriend Blair Waldorf pounces on him just as the infamous Serena turns up at the party; Nate is clearly keen to see Serena again and we immediately realise that Nate may have had a 'thing' for the blond Serena in the past. When Blair crosses the room to meet her supposed 'BFF' Serena, it's all vacuous, insincere air kisses and meaningless chit-chat. Nate's first love triangle is underway and the pilot is only a few minutes old!

The role of the Gossip Girl is pivotal to the entire show and we see that everyone is logging on to her website to keep up with the latest gossip, personal snippets, photos, rumours and so on. As with the show itself, most of the characters on-screen seem to want to deny they look at the site, but actually they love it! In fact, the abbreviations of the website referring to 'S' and 'B' etc. are used by most of the characters in real life too, confirming that they are all living out and/or catching up with the *Gossip Girl* blog.

The next scene in the pilot sees Nate and his long-time childhood friend Chuck Bass on a bus talking about a girl. Chuck – played by Ed Westwick of course! – is the dark foil to Nate's more honest personality. The way that Chuck describes 'violating' this one particular girl's innocence immediately appalls his friend Nate, setting out early on the very different moral values of the two pals. Nate, it seems, is clearly the All-American good guy; Chuck obviously isn't! Chace is brilliantly cast, as from a purely physical point of view he ticks every box in the stereotypical US definition of a hunk. The dynamic between Nate and Chuck underpins much of *Gossip Girl*, something we see very early on in the pilot: the contrasting moral values, the different styles, the totally different approach to women and so on. Despite all these differences, Nate and Chuck are very much a case of 'opposites attract'; their friendship is a deep and strangely reliant one.

With Blair trying to seduce Nate, he is now in a dilemma, with thoughts of the recently returned Serena in his mind. We soon discover that Nate and Serena had kissed at a wedding the previous year and that was why she had to leave town. The raunchy wedding scene of S and N kissing also sets the tone for the more explicit nature of the show, which would go on to cause much controversy and negative headlines. The revelation of the wedding kiss leads to Nate and Blair breaking up, which is not a popular move with his father, who is trying to negotiate a business deal with Blair's mother.

Nate is suppressed, suffocated, his father's money-making and power struggles obviously taking precedence over his needs. The viewer quickly feels sympathy for Nate, which only makes him even more endearing and attractive (Blair has an overbearing parent too!). He is immersed in but apparently not entirely comfortable with all the luxurious superficialities of life on the Upper East Side, and this theme is a recurring one that we see Nate struggle with – later in the first season he gets sucked into a gambling scam after being drawn towards a wealthy old school pal who appears to enjoy a more liberal life of travelling the world and being free of society's expectations.

Yet when Nate reassures Blair that he won't talk to Serena or even consider she exists any more, we all know this isn't going to happen! So Nate is lying, although at the time he says those words, he (kind of) believes them. The words will, of course, turn out to be completely hollow.

The pilot is very much focused on Nate/Chace and his relationship with Blair, Serena, his father and his sense of frustration at not being able to live his life as he wants. When Serena turns up at another party uninvited, it all kicks off, with Blair and Nate arguing again, everyone in the room checking their phones for text updates and Chuck hovering like a black widow spider over a young girl called Jenny. At the end of the pilot, a yellow cab drives off into the Manhattan night with Serena, Jenny and her brother Dan all safely inside, while Nate and Chuck watch, both with completely different agendas! It's a thrilling, compelling and addictive episode.

Chace was sure the pilot would lead to a full series: 'I was really impressed with the look and the music,' he told *MediaBlvd*. 'It was unbelievable. There's no weak links on anything, from the acting to the directing to the lighting. It all came together very nicely.' At the same time, looking back,

Chace thinks that the pilot was perhaps a little too raunchy, as he told www.thestar.com: 'They added a scene with my father to show where Nate is coming from. It's really not about sex as much as having too much of everything.'

The pilot also set a great precedent for the show's evocative soundtrack. Over the four seasons to date, there have been some great songs used to ramp up the atmosphere, with contributions from Rihanna, the late, great Amy Winehouse, Albert Hammond Jr. and Angels and Airwaves.

When the news came through that CW had decided to fund the entire series, it was a massive moment for Chace as well as all the other cast members. One practicality was that Chace had to relocate to New York for filming. He was thrilled to be in the Big Apple. Previously he'd only visited as a Texan tourist when he was just 16 and even then had only done all the obvious sight-seeing tours that you do on holiday. This time around, city life was a great new experience for Chace: 'I completely fell in love with New York when we were filming the pilot.' After filming he would party, eat at cool restaurants and shoot pool in cool bars with his friends, so it's perhaps not hard to see why the city holds such a big attraction for him! He loves the fact that you can get food 24/7, he enjoys the city's famous street corner hot dog stands and when he was chatting to one interviewer about being fairly rudimentary at cooking, co-star Ed Westwick butted in and pointed out he was missing a trick: 'It's about knowing how to pick up the phone and order something!'

Even before the first episode of *Gossip Girl* aired, the hype surrounding the show and the stellar reputation of the writers and producers suggested that it was about to be a massive smash hit. Chace was acutely aware of this yet was disarmingly honest about the effects and repercussions this might have on his life, as he told *MediaBlvd*: 'I'm not prepared at all, to be honest. I'm taking it day by day. It's insane. I want to take it episode by episode and just make sure my work is good. The rest, I hope, will take care of itself.'

Chace fans didn't have to wait long for the first glimpse of their man. Nate/Chace appears nearly seven minutes into the first episode, woken by a phone call from Blair to remind him of the brunch event. It turns out he is in the same room as Chuck who has been kept company by two women, while Nate has slept alone on the couch! They chat about the night before and it's clear that the two mates are somehow a perfect foil for each other. Chace heads off to the brunch in full dinner jacket attire, bumping into Serena's mother and doing a very bad job of trying to be indifferent about her daughter. The N S B love triangle takes on a new angle when Serena's new date, Dan, and Nate realise that they are both chasing her affections. At the climactic brunch later, Serena and Nate secretly meet up – with Nate again wearing a designer suit – but Blair invites herself too and there is yet another argumentative confrontation. As the opening episode closes, it is revealed that Serena slept with Nate at last year's wedding after all, and a fight ensues when Chuck calls Dan's sister a slut. Nate exits the episode with his relationship with Blair nearly in ruins, lying next to her in bed attempting to reconciliate. Not for the first time, we witness Blair and Nate's on-off relationship spiral out of control. With Blair holding Chace/Nate's hand as the end music starts to roll, the first episode of *Gossip Girl* leaves a lot of questions unanswered. Serena ends the episode by binning her mobile, but it clearly won't prove to be so easy to lose her connections with the Upper East Side elite.

Chace was quite literally an unknown before that debut episode aired. Yet by then, anticipation for the new show had reached sufficient heights that his celebrity was almost running away from the reality. Writing for thestar.com, Jim Bawden said: 'These are Chace Crawford's last, precious days of anonymity. There will now be a moment's silence for you to ask: "Who the heck is Chace Crawford?" Tune in tonight on the CW and you won't have to ask again.'

Chace himself seemed equally unaware of what was about to happen – namely that his life would never be the same again. In one sense, this was never inevitable as each year many new TV series are piloted and debuted and most fall by the wayside; however, there was an endearing naïveté to his apparently blissful innocence: 'I really don't know what to expect.' He also admitted to last-minute nerves: '[It's] nerve-racking,' he told thestar.com. 'It puts on a lot of pressure. You have to prepare for either outcome. Whether it's a flop from the hype or it lives up to the hype. I'm completely confident in it though.'

Gossip Girl was quickly being tagged as '*The* OC Goes East' but what started off initially as a flattering comparison would soon turn into an outdated parallel, as *Gossip Girl* became an instant ratings smash. Reviews were brilliant with many focusing on Chace's performance; the following day, the opening episode of *Gossip Girl* was being talked about all over America. One thing was immediately clear: the CW network had a major hit on their hands.

However, with an entire season to shoot, no one had time to rest on their laurels and toast the huge success of the opening episode. Filming often spilled out on to the streets of the world's biggest film set, Manhattan. Initially there had been talk of filming in Vancouver or even possibly Los Angeles, but with the Big Apple taking such a prominent role in the show, the producers decided to plump for the real deal. They used the same stages as had been utilised by the award-winning *Sopranos* and as such the show has a very authentic feel.

With many of the young cast being unknowns, these early days of filming were a simple pleasure. Chace was unashamed about his relative inexperience: 'It's all new to me. The younger actors are sticking together – it's the only way to survive the craziness. Right now we can shoot in Central Park and nobody bothers us.' Not for long …

Working with the two famous TV geniuses Schwartz and Savage was a real pleasure for Chace, as he told Josh Clinton:

'Oh man, they're great. They were on every day for the pilot and were there for the first few episodes ... Josh was the youngest television creator ever at 26 when he created *The OC*. It's so cool. They have the lingo down, they have the cutting-edge writing that flows like butter. It's unbelievable. It's been great ... Stephanie is so great. You can always call her up and count on her help. They are always so conducive to what you want to do. We all hang out when they are in town, so it's like a big family.'

As the show's fame accelerated in those heady first few weeks of broadcast, quiet days out filming in Manhattan became a thing of the past. Pretty soon, the security around the shoots was manic: 'Yeah, it can be rather difficult,' Chace explained to *TV Interviews* magazine, 'but we're all used to it ... It can be annoying on location when photographers are in your line of vision, snapping away. They're like little wasps that fly around you! It's also funny with girls – sometimes, after 3.30 p.m. when school's gone out, if one of them sees you, the viral text messaging starts! Then after an hour you turn around and there's like 100 of them ... with their moms. It's pretty cool though.' He also noticed that it wasn't just the obvious teenage girl fans who were coming along to the filming either; over time, as the show's profile grew, he started to spot wealthy Upper East Side New Yorkers – namely the very same people the show was fictionalising – coming along to watch too.

To be fair, his own mum had also visited the city 'to see what all the fuss is about!' Endearingly, Chace took her to eat at Butter, a restaurant/bar that features in *Gossip Girl*, and later took her to some other local bars because she'd said she wanted him to 'show me one of those little *Gossip Girl* places!'

Chace loves walking around the city – although NY is crammed with traffic, Chace will stroll around and enjoys the fact he doesn't always need to drive. He's also on record saying he finds the diversity of the Big Apple very appealing and has learned a lot from being around so many different cultures compared to the more conservative lifestyle usually found in Texas. 'It's infectious, it's a change of pace for me.' He's also said, 'New York's a big playground. I have a bike, and I'm really into just being outside. Especially in the summertime. The winters could eventually get to me [though], I mean, I'm a southern boy, so I like that humidity!'

Intriguingly, although he was now well aware of the huge fan base surrounding the original books, he seemed reluctant to immerse himself too much in the paper version of *Gossip Girl*, as this quote from the *Boston Herald* suggests:

'I actually thought I owed it to the fans to read [the books]. I got halfway through the first one and realised we can do something else, take it where we want it to go. And I feel like the show is going to be able to stand on its own. We know the gist of our characters and know how it's supposed to be. I feel personally it kind of gets in my head if I read all twelve [books] or whatever there are.'

Actually Chace was not alone, with several of the key actors and actresses admitting that they hadn't read the series; most had in fact read some or all of the first book only. 'The books put a little bit of pressure on the expectations and all that jazz,' admitted Chace to *The CW Source*.

Back on the show, Nate's life is nothing if not a roller coaster. After the tumultuous introduction of the pilot and first episode, life doesn't get any easier for Chace's character. He seems incapable of making a final decision between Blair and Serena and it begins to feel like he wants whichever one he cannot have. Chace's fan base forgive him this indecision of course and from the writers' point of view, it allows *Gossip Girl* to repeatedly run the 'will they, won't they?' storyline that is so captivating to fans.

Nate/Chace's relationship with Chuck is also a complex one and as Season 1 progresses it becomes ever more complicated when Chuck sets his lecherous eyes on Blair. To be fair, Nate had messed Blair around a lot, so there could be no complaints, particularly as Nate had slept with Blair's own best friend Serena. The circles of love interest get ever more complicated and messy with each episode. Yet even after an affair with Blair, Chuck and Nate holiday in Monaco, for ever linked (although at this point Nate is oblivious to Chuck's deceit). Inevitably the secret gets out and a fight leaves Nate with neither his girlfriend nor his best friend. Again the show plugs sympathy for Nate before Season 1 ends with Chuck and Nate reconciled, that strange, intimate bond reaffirmed. Millions of Chace Crawford fans watched every episode obsessively and no doubt all were thinking how great it would be to offer him a shoulder to cry on!

So the first season of *Gossip Girl* was a huge smash hit. The Internet was buzzing with talk of the characters, the actors and actresses, the gossip, the clothes, every aspect of the show was being dissected and discussed. Only a few short months earlier Chace had been a relative unknown auditioning hopefully for the role of Nate Archibald. Yet by Christmas of 2007, he was one of the biggest new names in television. And there was far, far more to come ...

CHAPTER 5

Loaded With Fame

WITH CHACE'S TV PROFILE now so high due to the meteoric success of the first season of *Gossip Girl*, any film roles he undertook were bound to attract intense interest from the public and media alike. Next up on the big screen for him was *Loaded*, starring opposite Jesse Metcalfe in a film produced by Wingman Productions and directed by Alan Pao (*The Art of Travel*, *Strike*).

Jesse Metcalfe was a similarly feted and good-looking young actor who had found fame in the daytime drama *Passions* and then most notably on the ABC TV drama *Desperate Housewives*. His first movie role had been in *John Tucker Must Die*, so in a sense he was only slightly ahead of Chace in career terms. The cast also boasted soccer player turned actor Vinnie Jones, who had made his name playing for the famously brutal Wimbledon FC but after his retirement from football had successfully made a big name for himself in Hollywood with superb performances in films such as *Lock, Stock and Two Smoking Barrels* and *Gone in 60 Seconds*.

Loaded is set around the dark and sinister edges of the LA club scene. Metcalfe's character Tristan Price leads a privileged life and has a loving family but he becomes increasingly involved in a dangerous web of drugs and crime. Initially he is introduced as a 25-year-old wealthy UCLA student with a high-flying career in law ahead of him, but one night after his birthday party he heads into the city to a go-go club ... and from then on his life starts to unravel. First off he hooks up with an unsavoury girl at the club which leads him to be reacquainted with an old college friend (and now big-time drug dealer) Sebastian Cole (Corey Large). As the drug lord abuses his 'friendship' with Tristan to access the latter's wealthy family and friends, events spiral into a mess of guns, violence and increasingly desperate actions.

Chace appears as Hayden Price, the younger brother of Jesse Metcalfe's character. Again Chace's role was somewhat peripheral and his actual amount of screen time rather limited. In one scene when Chace and his character's girlfriend are smooching in a car, they are accosted by Johnny Messner's character and beaten up. The veteran actor played a neat trick on the pair of young stars by acting in character and genuinely intimidating them, so that the tension and fear on-screen became palpable. The scene is really quite uncomfortable and the violence and cruelty shown is disturbing – when his character Hayden is threatened by his neck being throttled, Chace seems genuinely short of breath and there is a real sadistic edge to the footage. Chace found it a strange experience but a brilliant learning curve: 'It was definitely one of the weirdest mixes of emotions I'd ever felt. I was really kinda pissed at him for a while. In the scene, it hurt! You can really imagine … it really affected me.'

Regardless of his modest role, Chace clearly made a good impression on set. One of his co-stars, Monica Keena, was quoted as saying, 'I don't know how somebody that good-looking can still be so nice!' while Nathalie Kelley said he was going to be the next Brad Pitt!

The filming of the entire movie only took one month and that fast-paced momentum is definitely captured on the screen, as the energy and edge on set translates into the finished article. Chace and Jesse became good pals during the shoot and have remained friends since.

The film itself was a so-called 'straight to DVD' release, meaning it never had widespread cinematic distribution, generally regarded within Hollywood as the mark of an inferior project. Reviews for the movie are certainly rather mixed. On realmovienews.com, the writer said that,

'The filmmakers ask for a bit too much forgiveness of the viewer … this creates a feeling of disbelief in both the driving plot and the other characters' insistence that they were not a part of Sebastian's larger plan. The script feels reminiscent of *The Hand That Rocks the Cradle*, *The Game*, and *Unlawful Entry*, and does not seem to add much originality to an already saturated genre.' In this review, like many others, Chace was not even mentioned. There were some positives however, such as this from *Sky Movies*: '[*Loaded*] goes off the rails to crowd-pleasing effect in a pacy ride that delivers its thrills with a glossy sheen.'

However, there was the overall sense that *Loaded* did not really take Chace's movie career forward. With *Gossip Girl* showing no signs of slowing down in ratings, there were clear indications that for now at least, Chace's small-screen profile was far bigger than his silver-screen persona.

Back at *Gossip Girl* Central, there were no such worries about mediocre reviews or limited commercial appeal. The show, even in its downtime, was creating a buzz on the Internet that was almost unprecedented. Fans of the show bought into the blogging focus of the narrator and there wasn't a day went by that a new site or blog influenced by the show was started. And more often than not, one character that everyone mentioned was Nate Archibald! As a consequence, Chace Crawford's fame quite literally exploded. In the aftermath of *Gossip Girl*'s first season, Chace realised that his life would never be the same again.

The most obvious reflection of the show's success was the huge number of fans who would turn up at any filming on the streets of Manhattan. While Chace was trying to work he would be bombarded with gifts and very often the screams of his fans would mean retakes. He constantly receives the more 'regular' fan worship presents – underwear, cuddly toys, food, pictures and letters – but he has also mentioned that one letter from a French fan that talked about how much the character of Nate meant to her was so touching that he kept it as a personal memento. Of course it works both ways and fans are desperate for items of his clothing, a clump of hair (!) or even on one occasion his half-drunk can of Coke. 'One day some girls formed a sort of doughnut shape, like a mob,' he told *Newsbeat*. 'We were trying to get to set and it was a bad time of day, 3.30 on a Friday when school was out. They all texted their friends and everyone came down. They were clawing at the clothes, they wanted [my] tie or Diet Coke can or anything. I had a lot of marriage proposals that day too, which was kind of funny.'

As the momentum behind *Gossip Girl* gathered pace, Chace noticed that it wasn't just young girls who wanted his attention, as this quote from *Vman* shows:

'I'll be out on the golf course, and some guy will come up to me, sort of sheepishly, and be like, "Hey, my wife really loves the show. Can I get a picture with you?" They're always super embarrassed. And I'm like, "C'mon man, you love the show." Women get their husbands or boyfriends sucked into it. I like to see that.' Chace himself also liked the idea of older fans, as he told *Extra*: '[The fan base] has changed a bit in that we have more fun with everyone ... it's nice to hear it from the adults, the older crowd ... '

A second aspect of the huge success of *Gossip Girl* and its impact on Chace's life is the massive volume of magazine, TV and radio interviews he has to do. At times, this can be exhausting but, along with Ed Westwick, Chace is one of the show's best promoters. Almost every interview asks him if he is single, who the hottest girl on set is and what's his dream date, his favourite look in a girl, his chat-up lines etc. He always seems to answer fairly diplomatically when it comes to 'Who is the best kisser on set?', choosing not to stoke the fires of any gossip about behind-the-scenes relationships. However, patient as he is, it must eventually get tiring to keep answering these sorts of questions.

It's noticeable that many interviewers meet him in the flesh and comment on his electric blue eyes (later, when he was filming a movie called *Twelve*, none other than 50 Cent was so impressed by the luminescence of his eyes that he called them 'Skyline eyes'). Mind you, other journalists comment as much about his 'trademark' bushy eyebrows! When he was a kid his mum used to occasionally tell him to pluck them but he says he doesn't like to be too preened and fake. Chace is clearly even more striking in person – in one interview with a British newspaper, the female journalist met Chace in a café and said that when he entered the room, there was an audible sigh of 'Aaaaahhhhh' from the women at various tables nearby.

Chace begins his modelling career very young!

Chace was a modest, popular teenager at school and a strong sportsman who would go on to be awarded 'Best Dressed' in his senior year.

Classic Chace Crawford, those eyebrows, that hair!

The obvious friendship and camaraderie between Chace and Ed Westwick persuaded the pals to rent an apartment together for maximum *Gossip Boys* fun.

Having fun on set with *Gossip Girl* co-star Blake Lively, and her super-cute pup, Penny.

Good looks run in the family! Here is Chace with his grandmother and mum.

As Nate Archibald in *Gossip Girl*, Chace wears some of the finest designer suits and formalwear.

Opposite: Chace is very close to his sister, Candice. Here they are together at a party at the White House.

Chace pictured on set in 2011 with Liz Hurley, a photo which sent the GG blogs crazy!

Another reporter asked him the same question three times because when he answered, she was just sitting there, looking at him.

Due to the online nature of the show's success, a lot of promotion is on the web which Chace also enjoys. However, he tries to steer clear of the countless blogs – at the time of writing there are over 100 Facebook fan groups about the show – as he says these will sometimes be filled with 'hate'. Endearingly, he kept his Facebook and Myspace accounts open after his fame broke on *GG*, but soon realised that this was impossible to continue and eventually closed them all down. Since those innocent days he has recoiled completely from an online public presence: 'I'm the biggest believer in not talking,' he told Christopher Bollen. 'I don't Twitter or MySpace or Facebook. I want to keep to myself. I don't want to be out there. You have to keep some kind of control over who you are.' Given the intrusion into his private life that his fame has inevitably attracted, this instinct to be more insular is likely to just become even more important to him.

Chace's profile is such that he also has many YouTube and related clips online; indeed, several fans have compiled their own montages of Chace clips. There are even clips specifically about intimate aspects of his career and life, so for example you have one such snip called 'Private pictures of Chace and Ed'.

After the initial joyous naïveté of his early comments on fame had subsided, and it became clear that the sheer scale of his celebrity was starting to invade his privacy, he acknowledged that at times his success was having a negative impact on his 'normal' lifestyle.

Chace has to balance promoting the show and his films with what must be an ever-increasing invasion into his private life. So across the hundreds of interviews he does each year, we find out more and more of the minute detail about Chace's personal life: what his worst habit is (talking loudly on the phone), what skincare products he uses ('a good face wash by SkinCeuticals'), how he gets that famous hairstyle (Bumble and Bumble Styling Wax), and the fact he prefers dry shaving to wet. He wears Right Guard deodorant, prefers texting, boxers and stubble, but doesn't like nose-piercings on a girl or 'alien' sunglasses like the ones Paris Hilton wears. He likes fishing trips and mountain biking with friends, blondes *and* brunettes, and booty shorts worn with high socks. He's good at Wii tennis, but also loves Trivial Pursuit and Scrabble, he's good at grilling chicken and prefers loafers to cowboy boots.

It wasn't just what we knew about his tastes and preferences either, living a normal life day-to-day was becoming increasingly difficult. With paparazzi following his every move, someone even posted his home address on the Internet. Speaking to *ES* magazine, he said:

'I don't want to sound like I'm bitching, but it's gotten more difficult to connect with people on that innocent, level playing field … The process of meeting people has gotten pretty abstract. It could be a bit of paranoia thrown in there on my side, just being wary of other people's intentions, or people having preconceived notions of who I am.'

Reflecting on his rapid success, Chace has said that he thinks his 'cynical attitude' helped, in that he carried with him a realistic philosophy on his chances of success. He was naturally quite wary of the 'celebrity' folk. The super-celebrity that Chace experienced was 'overnight' in many ways, but that was also the case for much of the cast. He feels that his co-stars have coped well with the surge of fame and media attention. It's hard to overestimate just how big *Gossip Girl* became and how fast!

When *New York* magazine ran a cover feature on *Gossip Girl*, the tag line was 'Best Show Ever'. In another notable interview the strapline gave a fair indication of how Chace had gone from new face to new star in a matter of months, as it hailed, 'The hottest new property in Hollywood right now'. It helped that he was openly single, keeping the hopes and dreams of his ever-growing legion of fans alive. However, he was clearly slightly wary of the whole 'hunk' tag: 'It's weird you know, I still don't know what a heart-throb is. No one's yet managed to tell me exactly what that is. But it's really cool – I mean, I can't say that I don't like some of the attention but I just want to focus on my career now and I haven't really bought into the whole Hollywood scene.' By now Chace was considered among the most desirable actors on the planet.

Perhaps unusually for such a famous face, as his fame escalated he has found himself being drawn back to his roots because he finds a certain reassurance in the people back in Texas, especially girls; his male pals like to remind him of his background whenever he goes back there and he's even attended international PR interviews suffering from sore red marks on his face where they had ruthlessly paintballed him the previous weekend! Chace is known to be very grounded – entertainment lore tells us that it is often the stars who enjoy the most rapid rise to fame that are most likely to implode. So with Chace having gone from aspiring actor to one of the hottest names in Hollywood in a few short months, it might be harder than you think to keep a reality check. One aspect of his life that certainly helps him here is his on-going friendships with pals from his childhood. He is still very close with people who have known him when he was just a kid at summer camp trying to get his first kiss. 'I've had the same friends since school,' he told *Ladmag*, 'and they find it so weird. I went to this amazing party a while ago and asked one of my best friends, Jason, if he wanted to come along. He was totally stoked but had no way of getting there, so I was like, "No problem, I'll send my car." So this amazing car picks him up from his house and drives him across the country to an incredible manor house and the paps are going mad as he gets out of the car with flash bulbs going off all around. He was like, "Duuuudde! What *is* this?!"' When he turned 24, Chace flew loads of his old college pals up to NYC, then on to the nearby resort of Watermill by private jets where they then stayed over for a weekend-long party. They were all fed by a private chef and also chartered a speedboat and kayaks.

Chace makes no secret of the fact he still loves to visit home; every summer he returns to his grandparents' lake house north of Texas and messes about on the water with his sister and her BFFs. The only real downside to fame with his old mates is that sometimes they might be a little uneasy around his good looks! 'Some of my friends now are a bit funny when I'm hanging out with them and their girlfriends. They just give that look that says, "Chace, don't even try." They've no reason not to trust me, but they still give me that look.'

Given that only a few years earlier he was an unknown at university, it must be fairly mind-boggling for Chace to see billboards with his photo twenty feet high or read stories in national magazines and newspapers about himself, especially when many of these reports are completely fabricated, as he told *Vman*. 'If I'm standing next to a dog, they'll say we're dating. Or next to my sister – I got that as well. I let it roll off my back. There's a lot of speculation with no reality to it, complete fabrications about my private life. My close friends and my family – ha! – they obviously know what the reality of my private life is. It's just comical.'

One obvious upside of his celebrity was the number of awards he would soon start to win. Fast-forward to Season

3 of *Gossip Girl* where we find the most obvious and biggest profile accolade that Chace has won to date regarding his looks, namely the 2009 'Hottest Bachelor' gong from *People* magazine. Although the trophy might sound rather trite, it is in fact a massively influential poll and previous winners have generally enjoyed great publicity as a result (*American Idol* winner Taylor Hicks, Matthew McConaughey and Mario Lopez are three examples). The award came with a front cover feature too and was a very high-profile recognition of Chace's new-found fame. Teasingly, he ambiguously told the magazine that, 'I'm not *not* looking for a girlfriend – but I'm not particularly looking for a girlfriend, either.'

Despite his modesty, he was openly thrilled by the award. Speaking to Ryan Seacrest on the latter's KIIS-FM radio show, Chace said, 'We were trying to watch the college games last night. Me and my friends are flipping through and [on] *Access Hollywood*, they're like x-ing out the other guys. When they're x-ing out [George] Clooney, that's when it hit me. I go, "Wow, that feels pretty surreal."' Chace also revealed that he had only told his parents in advance about the award: 'It's such a big deal. It's funny I didn't really realise how massive [it] was going to be.' He has won other relatively prestigious awards too, such as the Teen Choice Award for 'Breakout TV Star' in 2008.

And just how did this 'hottest bachelor' maintain his fabulous physique? 'I'm a big gym frequenter,' he told blockbuster.co.uk, 'I guess I got it from playing sports in Texas. I played football from fifth grade onwards so working out was part of my lifestyle. My sister is a personal trainer and my dad and mom go to the gym so it's kind of a family thing. It's a way of life, a lifestyle.' Mind you, he seems to have to work hard at not eating junk food, as this fun quote from the promotion of *Covenant* is anything to go by! Asked what superpowers he would most like to have and how he would use them if he was a real-life warlock like his character Tyler, he said, 'I would abuse my body and eat McDonald's, then use my powers to decrease the fat!' (he later retracted this opinion somewhat after watching *Supersize Me*!). That said, he also suggested, 'There would be no such thing like taxes or speeding tickets for me ever again.' He's also on record as saying, 'There's nothing sexier than a Big Mac. I don't eat a lot of them, but it's just a whole complete package.'

Even though Chace was always conspicuously grateful for the awards and props he got for his looks, he was also always a little uneasy about being taken too lightly: 'I'm trying everything I've got to struggle against that stereotype,' he modestly told the Canadian edition of *TV Guide*. 'As far as the sex symbol thing goes, I'm not ready for any of that. To be labelled that, I guess, is an honour, but it doesn't give me any sort of validation. I gauge myself when I see the work being done.'

Speaking in *VMan* he reiterated his awareness of being 'pigeon-holed': 'There are a lot of adverse effects of being a certain type, which I am. Look, I wouldn't be in the business if I didn't feel I had what it takes to have longevity. Everyone has a certain castability (sic), or quality they're always going to have to fight. I think the best remedy is to reinvent yourself. I'm not going to take the same type of role in the future.'

At times his wariness at being typecast spills over into his 'day job' at *Gossip Girl*. Referring to scenes where he takes off his shirt, he told *OK!* that,

'I like to keep it as few and far between as I can. I mean, I don't want to be a shirtless whore! I don't want to come across as a himbo – is that what you call it? But it's part of my job, it's probably going to plague me for ever. There was an episode where we were crashed out on the sofa after a big night out and they wanted me to wake up in boxers, so I argued with them about it, I mean, first of all, who gets wasted with their buddy and smokes weed and then strips down to their boxers before they pass out on the couch?! No one does that. Why am I naked on my buddy's couch? It was weird so I fought it.'

His movie idols were partly responsible for this slight reticence; Leonardo DiCaprio, River Phoenix and Paul Newman all had phases of their careers where their stunning looks threatened to choke off a variety of roles and so Chace is understandably conscious that the same does not happen to him.

It was a sign of his considerable fame that by May 2009, Chace, along with Ed Westwick, was invited to attend The

White House Correspondents' Dinner – a celebrity-drenched occasion that on that night also saw such famous faces as Ben Affleck, Eva Longoria and John Cusack among the 2,000 or so guests.

Impressively, as Chace has acclimatised himself to the white-hot spotlight of fame, he has impressively started to use his celebrity to good effect too. This is the reason he involved himself in a campaign and TV advert for teensforjeans.com and dosomething.org, a campaign designed to get people donating their old branded jeans to raise funds for homeless charities. The power of a famous face such as his can fuel donations and awareness of such charities beyond all expectations and Chace was keen to make sure that his new-found celebrity was always maximised for good causes.

It has inevitably taken Chace some time to get used to the fame game, but he doesn't complain in interviews and even when a private dinner or party is interrupted by photographers there are never reports of him lashing out or moaning about his life. This is one star who seems very happy with his success. And regardless of the ups and downs of his new fame, in just a few short months Chace Crawford had become one of the most sought after new actors on the planet.

CHAPTER 6

'Have You Met My Friend Chuck?'

2008 WAS A BUSY year for Chace as alongside *Loaded* it also saw another movie role, this time in the supernatural flick – billed as 'a tweener horror' – called *The Haunting of Molly Hartley*. The lead role of Molly was played by Haley Bennett and fellow CW star AnnaLynne McCord was also cast as one of the 'bad girls'. The film was ambitiously described by one source as '*Carrie* for the *Gossip Girl* generation', a reference to the seminal Stephen King horror flick that to this day is one of the greatest scary movies ever made.

The film opens with a shocking scene – an unknown girl is meeting her boyfriend in a wooden shack in a forest, only for her father to interrupt them and insist she comes home with him. Clearly a troubled dad, in the subsequent argument on the journey he discovers they intend to get married, but then inexplicably spins the car only for it to be hit by a huge truck. With Molly lying badly injured but still alive, her father then takes a shard of windscreen and stabs her to death, while mysteriously saying, 'I can't let you turn 18, I couldn't let them take you.'

Fast-forward to the present day and the central character of the film is a college-age Molly who is suffering from recurring and very frightening nightmares ahead of going to her expensive new private school. The film is nearly twelve minutes in before Chace's character Joseph makes his appearance, a pupil reading monotonously from *Paradise Lost*. When he smiles at Molly, it's clear from the resulting ruffles around the girls in the classroom that he is the subject of much female attention. In this role he looks very young, especially bearing in mind he is six or seven years older than his character.

While Molly struggles to settle into her new school, Joseph is one of her few allies – seemingly – although the preponderance of 'evil whispering' in dark corners suggests there is more at play here than just Molly's first-term nerves. This is reinforced by her nose bleeds and severe panic attacks – usually induced by malevolent spirits – again with Chace/Joseph as her main source of support. Chace's appearances in the film are relatively limited, usually as a smouldering shoulder to cry on.

As the film progresses we discover that Molly's mother appears to be mentally ill, and there is a particularly harrowing 'flashback' scene in the bathroom when she attacked and attempted to kill her daughter by stabbing her in the chest with a pair of scissors. Her mother was subsequently locked up as a potential paranoid schizophrenic or psychotic, and the hereditary component of these diseases plays on the young Molly's mind. For Chace's young, predominantly teenage fan base, no doubt these scenes were rather more harrowing than they were perhaps used to seeing in *Gossip Girl*!

Molly's apparitions of her mother become increasingly disturbing and she appears to be spiralling into a madness of her own. We eventually learn that Molly's parents made a pact with a mysterious 'religious nutcase' – a foil for the devil – in a hospital corridor when their unborn child was miscarried: in return for saving the newborn's life, the devil would take over her soul when she turned 18. Her parents' attempts to kill Molly are merely designed to 'save' her from a life spent in the service of the devil. Her mother reveals that this was not the only baby to have been a part of such a pact.

An escalating series of events including numerous deaths ramp up the tension as Molly's life falls apart. Molly confides in Chace/Joseph that she believes she is about to be handed over to the devil – rather than being mentally ill and deluded – and he offers to take her away from it all, looting his father's safe deposit box and eloping. Chace's role never really progresses much beyond the handsome male love interest … until the climax of the film when it is revealed that he too is in league with the devil. In theory, being presented with a birthday cake near to midnight on your 18th birthday by Chace Crawford would normally be a pleasant surprise, but in this case he is standing next to a large knife and is soon accompanied by numerous dark shadows, representing equally corrupt souls. Some people might say that Nate Archibald was equally evil at times, although perhaps Chuck Bass would have been a fairer comparison! The film ends with her bleeding father being dragged in only for Molly to be offered the chance to kill him to redeem the situation and break the pact; instead she stabs herself, but it's too late as the clock has passed midnight. Her suicide attempt fails, she cannot be killed and the devil has won her soul.

Disappointingly, Chace has no dialogue in the film's big climax when the 'reveal' is made that he too is an acolyte of the devil, instead he stands in the shadows looking gorgeous but saying nothing. The film closes with Molly in a mental ward but she is visiting her father, not as a patient herself. She turns her back on him and walks away for ever, later to be seen as a teacher inspiring a new intake of pupils ... who are all blissfully unaware that their mentor works for the devil.

Part of Chace's motivation to take the role was a desire to find a film similar to *American Beauty*, which he rates as one of the greatest films ever made (and his own personal all-time favourite). 'I want to do the edgy independent movies, like DiCaprio did,' he told *VMan*, 'but you have to balance it out,' he says. 'It's about carving out your leading-man role. *Fight Club*? Yes! *X-Men*? Yes! All sorts of different films. *American Beauty*? Yes!' He is also a fan of cool directors such as Cameron Crowe, Quentin Tarantino and Martin Scorsese.

The Haunting of Molly Hartley employed many staple horror movie tricks such as unseen 'screeching' evil spirits, scary dreams and flashbacks, hand-held distant footage etc. and was not perceived by most critics to have broken any new ground. The characterisation was criticised as formulaic and the screenplay derided too. Notably, for the movie's promotional poster, Chace's face was bigger than any of his co-stars'. Released suitably at Halloween, the movie was received well by only a handful of critics; however, the majority were less than charitable. Blog.moviefone.com said, 'It's as if the filmmakers sought to strip the story of every possible nuance and make something that was truly generic. I've read fortune cookies that were scarier, not to mention smarter and more interesting.' However, similarly to *Loaded* before it, *The Haunting of Molly Hartley* had a very limited commercial impact – although this time the film was released to cinemas, it was in a small number only and soon after went on to DVD.

Despite his best efforts, some critics pointed out that Chace was already playing very similar roles each time: teenage hunks, usually not the alpha male types, slightly shy, often troubled. Of course he also played drug dealers (!) but again there was an element of the troubled soul even there. For *The Haunting of Molly Hartley* he was in a private school uniform, so the 'stereotype' comment was even easier to make. For

Chace, this was another disappointing film project; he still seemed to struggle to land a role in a movie that won the critics' and public's hearts.

With *Gossip Girl's* success continuing unabated, Chace and Ed became closer friends – swapping jokes at press junkets, going out on the town together and generally living the highlife as two 20-something men would.

Realising they hit it off so well, they decided to share an apartment – which of course the fan sites loved. It was a practical decision as much as two mates moving in together: not knowing whether *Gossip Girl* would have longevity as a show it made sense for the two to rent rather than buy.

Chace has since explained how the idea came about: 'We'd hung out a little while filming the pilot,' he explained to *People*, 'and we talked about it. So I called him up when he was back in London and said, "Hey, man, do you want to do this rooming thing?" He'd never lived away from home before. I had to tell the kid how to work a laundry machine!'

Chace says they lived together like brothers, arguing occasionally, drinking beers and playing pool, partying, and watching a lot of TV on a massive flat screen. He found the interest in the famous pair's intimate household habits rather bemusing; amidst rumours that the apartment was seeing its fair share of celeb parties and wild times, he said that: 'I don't know why anyone wants to read about the condition of our apartment. It cracks me up ... We have a few roof-deck parties from time to time, but that's all.' (If you had been invited to one of their parties, the music on the iPod would have included mainly rock such as Nirvana, the White Stripes, Audioslave, the Black Keys, The Racounteurs, Van Halen, Red Hot Chili Peppers and Guns N' Roses as well as a fair few Brit bands such as Kooks, Stereophonics and Oasis.)

Rumours circulated that Westwick and Crawford were especially messy but this was something that Chace denied strongly, saying this had come from people who'd not even set foot in their flat. 'Personally I'm obsessive-compulsive about the placement and cleanliness of my things,' he revealed to Christopher Bollen. 'But I'm not always the best, so I had a housekeeper come every two weeks. It was pretty immaculate, I have to say. It had its down points, but Ed and I ran a good ship there for a while.'

Living with an Englishman meant Chace found himself using various British phrases, such as 'rubbish' for garbage and 'garage' too. One of Chace's best friends is from Brighton so he was already pre-disposed to the accent! Funnily enough, the two hadn't hung out much during the filming of the pilot because Ed's girlfriend was staying over with him. But as soon as the main series started, they became pals and roomed together, and things changed: 'We went for it. You kind of become brothers in that sense. And we're going through a similar craziness of the show. We don't have the same hours – it's not like we have the same 9-to-5 job every day and work in the same cubicle! It's very lop-sided, in fact. It's a good situation and it's worked out well.'

Inevitably, and perhaps farcically too, their close friendship led to entirely incorrect and rather bizarre rumours that they were having a sexual relationship – something that Chace (and Ed!) strenuously denied but which still made him laugh with bewilderment. *Gossip Girl* has a very large gay following, which *Out* magazine described as a 'cultural phenomenon whose early adopters weren't actually teenage girls but rather gay men trapped in arrested development or seeking to vicariously prolong their youth.'

As major leads in the show and with the help of their stunning looks, clearly Ed and Chace had strong gay followings too and both had been interviewed by numerous gay and lesbian publications. And of course living together in that Chelsea, New York apartment together (an area which some publications called the ('"Gayborhood" of NYC') was also noted by some magazines. But *none* of the above suggests in any way that they are gay themselves! Chace told *People* magazine how the two friends were totally bemused and eventually became indifferent to the gossip: 'You know what we really did the first time we heard it? Ed goes, "Oh, did you hear that rumour about us being gay?" I was like, "Yeah, man." He starts laughing and we're kind of like, "Okay, you want to go play pool and have a beer?"'

Chace had always known that as his fame grew, so too would public fascination with his private life and therefore the chances of such rumours circulating began to increase. After all, this wasn't the only time that 'gay' rumours had been spread about Chace. In 2008, he and former *NSYNC boy-band star JC Chasez were also moved to dismiss the rumours that they were having a relationship. 'I don't care about [people's] assumptions or anything,' a clearly riled JC said to *People*, 'but when people outright lie, that's wrong. So I think that part of the rumour is outright stupid.' The apparent reasoning was that they had been photographed hanging out at Elton John's party and also one time in Las Vegas; Chace pointed out that 'I've probably hung out with JC three times in my entire life!'

As he often does, Chace dealt sublimely with the false rumours and used his modesty and humour to ridicule the ludicrous gossips; talking to *Details* magazine he laughed off the suggestions thus: '[I'm a] model turned actor, dime a dozen, eye candy, doesn't know what he's doing ... and Perez Hilton says I have "gayface". So on top of everything else, I have to overcome gayface.' He's also said that in a way you haven't really 'made it' until someone suggests you are gay and revealed that his very first thought when he heard the gay rumour was, 'That's a stretch!'

Interestingly, while he laughed off the gay rumours, there were other whispers about his fellow cast members that he was far more seriously disgusted with. After tabloid reports that certain *Gossip Girl* actors and actresses were divas and that the cat-fighting on set was out of control, Chace was clearly angry: 'It couldn't be more opposite from the truth. We really have a wonderful cast of actors ... there are no big egos, so that sorta nonsense irks me, because it detracts from who they are as real people.'

In 2009, the two pals decided it was finally time to get their own places. 'Frat time's over,' Chace told *People*, 'I needed my own space. [My new flat is] a little bit secluded and I like that ... I have my own privacy ... I found a nice Chipotle in the neighbourhood and that's all I need. I need my Chipotle and my little coffee maker and I'm good.'

Chace plumped for an apartment in the more low-key (and less touristy) financial district of the city. He revealed that he'd started buying minimalist leather furniture, a huge flat-screen TV and had ordered an espresso machine; he was looking forward to buying cool art for the walls and he also wanted to install a beer tap, preferably for Bud Light. Notably, when he finally made the move, his mum travelled up to NYC to help him out!

CHAPTER 7

The Celebrity Circus

SEASON 2 OF *GOSSIP Girl* is Chace/Nate's 'cougar' time, when it is revealed that he's been dating a much older woman. This led to hundreds of questions in interviews with Chace about whether he would consider a relationship with someone more mature. He was always diplomatic, perhaps aware that many *Gossip Girl* fans were of older years too! It also highlighted the increasing risk of fans and the media blurring the lines between fact and fiction, with the gay rumours and his cougar tastes all mixing up in the crazy whirlpool of Chace's ever-increasing fame! It wasn't just Chace either – the media were constantly trying to suggest that behind the scenes was just as gossip filled as in front of the camera. After all, with so many good-looking actors and actresses on board for the show, there were bound to be rumours about who was getting on particularly well with whom. Then there were the actual public relationships such as Ed Westwick and Jessica Szohr, which only whipped up the frenzy even more. Chace was regularly cornered about this 'on-set romance' question, but always seemed to wriggle out of a straight answer with some dignity! Usually he'd do so with humour, with quotes such as, 'I just hate everybody [on set], I'm just a loner!'

The second season also sees Nate's money cut off as his father has fled the country, but his lower income did little to quell Chace's growing popularity – if anything his financial predicament made Chace/Nate even more popular with his ever sympathetic fans. Again, Nate sometimes behaves in a way that if it were Chuck we would all be fuming, but somehow his character gets away with it due to his brilliant white smile and All-American beauty: when Dan takes him in and offers him a bed, his kindness is (inadvertently) thrown back in his face when Nate kisses Dan's sister Jenny. Not an ideal way of saying thanks to a good Samaritan but Nate seems to be able to act like this and get away with it!

Nate's friendship with Chuck is strengthened in this season too, but this is soured again later when Blair and Nate reconcile (once more!). And Nate's way of proving to Chuck and his recent belle Vanessa that he isn't in a relationship with Blair? He restarts his affair with Blair!

By the end of Season 2, Chace was a major TV star and *Gossip Girl* seemed unstoppable. Ever hungry for more success and always ambitious, Chace continued with an array of other projects unrelated to Nate Archibald's latest activities. One such project was a remake of the 1984 smash movie *Footloose*, which had originally starred Kevin Bacon. The tale of this

Chicago boy who inspires a town where music and dancing are illegal was a massive smash on its original release; the story was very loosely based on a real-life town in Oklahoma and Bacon's energy, fantastic dancing and on-screen charisma won over audiences around the globe. It has since been widely acknowledged as an iconic 1980s classic movie.

The original film had 'broken' Kevin Bacon as a worldwide star; it also starred Sarah Jessica Parker in one of her earliest film appearances and Madonna had even auditioned for the role played by Lori Singer – so it was clear that history suggested this film could turn an unknown or moderate star into a mega-star.

In the production chair for this re-make was Kenny Ortega (who was the man behind *High School Musical*), with shooting originally scheduled to start in March 2010. However, the film would become plagued by casting problems and delays. As well as a switch in director and scripts, there would be changes in key acting personnel too.

High School Musical heart-throb Zac Efron was initially lined up for the lead role of Ren McCormack – which would have given the project a global following immediately due to the multi-billion dollar success of *HSM* – but he eventually pulled out, with rumours suggesting he was concerned about being typecast so early in his career. After this news broke, speculation as to who would fill Kevin Bacon's dancing shoes was rife and it was perhaps a sign of his exploding fame that Chace's name was mentioned as a favourite. One rather fantastic rumour suggests that a key Hollywood executive asked his daughter about Chace taking over the lead role and her squeals of excitement and swooning over his name convinced them to approach the *Gossip Girl* hunk. For the successful audition, Chace sang the film's iconic signature tune with just a piano for accompaniment. Chace later revealed it was a very rigorous audition lasting over five hours!

Speaking to *Entertainment Weekly*, Chace said of the development: 'I know Zac and we're actually friends. He's gotta make the best choice for his career at this point and I have to make the best for mine and luckily it worked out for both of us.' When Chace was announced as the potential lead male, it seemed a very popular choice, with message boards and chat rooms delighting in the fact. Even Kevin Bacon's wife Kyra was openly pleased: 'We're thrilled! [Our daughter] Sosie is a big fan. We met him at the White House Correspondents' Dinner. Kevin and he had a chat. He's very sweet.' Her husband Kevin was quoted as saying he was really 'looking forward' to seeing Chace's efforts too. Those worried that Chace would have to wear very tight leggings and 1980s-style cut-off sweatshirts needn't have been concerned as the movie was a very modern update on the classic film.

Ahead of the first day of filming, Chace and the film's producers scheduled in nine months of intense preparation. As with *Covenant*, the physical demands of the new film were bound to be substantial and Chace happily admitted the early work was already proving very demanding: 'I've started prep for [the film] and I'm extremely sore! I've been training for days, but I'm extremely sore ... It's really intense. We're getting the gymnastics and doing some workouts. I'm learning some basic moves. I've got a little rhythm. I'm realising every day how much of all the nine months [of prep] I'm going to need.' As well as the obvious physical workouts and dance training (classical and modern such as break-dancing), Chace began two hours of daily martial arts training, as well as masses of stretching and gymnastics techniques. His core strength and flexibility were the key issues and as a result within a few weeks of training, his already toned physique was starting to look even more ripped. 'I'm getting muscles that I didn't even know were there!'

When a few critics raised eyebrows that a 'non-dancer' was going to play a role that was clearly technically very demanding, Chace confidently brushed these worries aside, with his tongue planted firmly in his cheek: 'There's this bar in New York City on the Lower East Side called the Darkroom,' he cheekily told *People* magazine. 'They have the best music, so a lot of us will go down there and just kind of let go. I've got some movement!' He was also happy to put his faith in the executives who had picked him: 'It's a risk because there are such high expectations for it. One of [them] produced the original movie and they also did *Chicago* so I'm kind of trusting them and listening to whatever they say.'

In a lengthy and very insightful chat with Christopher Bollen of *Interview* magazine, Chace seemed unfazed by the challenge ahead: 'I am confident because I knew I had rhythm – and I'm athletic. I know I have rhythm, I have it in my brain. And I'm a quick learner. I'm better at doing something by imitation than being told. So if I'm working with the dance coach who tries to explain it, I say, "Just do it and I'll get it." That's how we've been working. I'm taking these private lessons. It's been unbelievable.' Mind you, what many fans didn't know was that way back when he had started taking acting lessons, his mum had suggested he also take dancing lessons, but he only went to one class before vowing never to return! As for the vocal demands of the role, Chace was also unperturbed: 'I'm a habitual car singer,' Crawford told *Wonderland* magazine. 'I actually go karaoking all the time, We get pretty competitive.'

As it turned out, however, Chace wouldn't need any further prep after all because in early April 2009, it was announced that he was no longer going to play the lead role. The reason given was simply that with the huge success of *Gossip Girl* showing no signs of letting up, Chace simply wouldn't have the time to fulfil both roles. The original plan had been to fit the filming in between seasons three and four of *Gossip Girl* but ultimately this proved impossible (the film's director Kenny Ortega would also later withdraw from the Paramount movie). Chace's would-be co-star, *Dancing With the Stars* beauty Julianne Hough, finally starred opposite Kenny Wormald when the film was shot in the autumn of 2010, with the film set for a late 2011 release.

A much smaller but nonetheless fun little side project came along for Chace in early 2009 when he appeared in a video for a song by Brit singing sensation Leona Lewis. Chace's manager knew the manager of the British star and this led to another interesting little role for him after they all hooked up at a party in London while he was promoting *Gossip Girl* in the UK. Chace and Leona had bumped into one another on a number of occasions and become friends, so when she was in New York filming the video for her next single – 'I Will Be' – she just asked Chace outright if he'd like to appear. 'She's such a sweet girl and I love her music ... and there were [originally] no lines or anything, so it was more of a favour.'

The chanteuse had taken America by storm with her multi-platinum-selling album *Spirit* in 2007. In the ballad's promo, Chace played Leona's boyfriend. Filmed like *Gossip Girl* in the Big Apple on an icy cold December day, the pairing obviously attracted a lot of publicity – surely the whole point?! – and Chace really enjoyed himself. As it happened, Chace's character did have some dialogue at the start of the video as the two stars are seen in a car anxiously holding a bag, presumably filled with money, while police sirens and the noise of New York provide the background soundtrack. Leona tells him to leave, saying she can't stay and promising to meet him later, shoving the bag into his hands and pleading, 'Trust me, take this and go!' It's not exactly a fast getaway, however, as

Leona then sits on the bonnet of their car to sing a few lines of the first verse while Chace sits in the back, probably wondering if he's going to get arrested after all. However, all is well for Chace as Leona is clearly sacrificing herself so that he can escape, and she is later seen being accosted by an NYPD officer (played by Cedric Darius).

Of course, the rumour mills swung into action and suggested that the two were an item but this was just plain wrong; Chace was only on set for a few hours and when asked if he still hung out with Leona, he answered with a rather curious phrase, saying they were 'semi-friends'. Leona told the media that she turned down the chance to kiss Chace in the video because she didn't want to upset her long-term boyfriend. Rather splendidly, she was also reticent on whether Chace would be her 'type', telling *Sugar* magazine that, 'He needs roughing up a bit! He'd be a really pretty girl … He's so beautiful, I mean, look at him. But I just don't think of him like that.' For his part, he said they were good platonic friends and as Leona is not an actress, he could see how any kissing sequence could make her feel uncomfortable.

Of course, by now Chace was hot property and whoever he worked or partied with was bound to find themselves the subject of media gossip. The false rumours about Leona were not the first time Chace had seen his relationships plastered across the front pages. Back in the autumn of 2007, when he'd been seen out on the town with *American Idol* winner and country music singing sensation Carrie Underwood, the Hollywood rumour mill had swung into full action.

Carrie had won the huge reality show then gone on to become one of the world's biggest country and western singers, scooping multiple trophies and selling millions of records. Around the time she was linked to Chace, she'd also been open that she was in the mood for dating, having broken up with Dallas Cowboys star quarterback Tony Romo (who would later become engaged to Chace's sister Candice!): 'I'd like to have someone other than my mom to call when I have good news.'

Initially both parties remained tight-lipped about any relationship. Take this non-committal quote from Carrie: 'He's really cute. I've met him and he seems like a really nice guy. He's got cool hair, he's a nice height and he just has beautiful blue eyes.' For his part, Chace was on record as saying that he'd never watched *American Idol*!

When Carrie appeared on the *Ellen De Generes Show*, she responded coyly to questions about Chace saying that she would certainly make him some home-cooked food but only if she could get hold of his telephone number first! And she topped that off by saying that she would 'cook for anyone that would like me to cook for them.'

A month later it was Chace's turn on the same show and he too was grilled by the immensely likable host De Generes. She trumped the awkwardness with Carrie by screening a naked photo of Chace ... albeit when he was a baby! But Chace was far more uncomfortable when she then produced a photo of him with Carrie, visibly squirming before neatly ignoring her probing question altogether and saying rather feebly, 'I am trying to get a pet right now.'

Unconvinced, the tabloids started to trail the couple's nights out, following them to celebrity haunts such as Manhattan's Marquee nightclub, Justin Timberlake's restaurant Southern Hospitality and Gramercy Park Hotel's ultra-trendy Rose Bar. At the latter, an unnamed source said, 'At one point, they were holding hands, off to the side of the table, like they didn't want people to see.' Only four days after Chace had squirmed on Ellen's couch, they were seen out clubbing again at the Marquee – notably dancing closely in full view of the rest of the clubbers.

The media interest meant that anything they ate at a restaurant would be listed on the Internet within hours of their meal – so we know that at Timberlake's restaurant they chewed through barbecued wings and Grannie's Pecan Pie while drinking Bud Light; if he was seen supporting Carrie's own career, such as at the side of the stage during the filming of *Live With Regis and Kelly*, again it was on the web within minutes; when their co-stars were involved in their own PR for various projects, questions about the 'celebrity couple' would inevitably arise; each time they headed out on the town their clothes were analysed in minute detail, such as Carrie's 'jewel-embellished blue dress' or Chace's 'suit and skinny black tie'.

But then, after just over six months, the news started filtering out that the two stars had broken up – and rumours said it had all been terminated by text message (which in light of the *Gossip Girl* way of life seemed entirely appropriate). However, although the two friends confirmed the break-up, the 'text dumping' was a detail that Chace strongly denied. The *Extra* TV show had quoted Carrie as saying 'It was completely mutual. We broke up over text so … it's like "peace out".' Chace just laughed this off, saying it wasn't that simple. 'No one breaks up by text! … It was all absolutely misrepresented,' asserted Chace, and went on to deny that the pair had never spoken since. The pressures on the relationship of her constant travelling on tour and also both their very active and hectic schedules is thought to have been a major contributing factor to the split.

Speaking in April 2008, Carrie told *People* that, 'We've parted ways. I actually haven't spoken to him in over a month.' There were rather conflicting reports saying it was Carrie who 'broke' Chace's heart but also that it was the actor who had decided to break it off. Chace had flown to visit her, even been spotted at dates on her tour, so he was clearly very keen. In January though, Carrie had downplayed the relationship seemingly, when she said, 'I'm not serious with anybody.'

Speaking to his sister Candice, *People* magazine reported how Chace was doing in the immediate aftermath of the break-up from Carrie: 'He's doing okay through this whole ordeal. He was upset about the break-up. It's always hard when you lose a relationship.' She went on to say that he and Carrie were still very good friends and the fact that there appears to have been no animosity is reinforced by Candice saying she thought Carrie was 'a doll'.

Reflecting later on the high-profile relationship, Chace was clearly shocked by the level of media interest in their partnership. 'I wasn't ready for all that craziness,' he later told *New York* magazine. 'I didn't realise what that was going to entail.' He elaborated on this in another interview saying, 'I have nothing bad to say about that experience. It was awesome. I just didn't know how to deal with it. I learnt a ton about dating someone in that kind of spotlight. It was such a whirlwind, but no regrets.' Carrie was similarly philosophical: 'I'm good alone for a while. It's been a while since I've just been single and free.' Chace also said that he was busy dating his punch bag and getting into spectacular shape for work!

If Chace thought the end of his relationship with Carrie Underwood would mark the end of the media and public's interest in his private life, he couldn't have been more wrong. His profile was now so high that any girl he was seen out on the town with became an immediate source of speculation. This aspect of his fame and good looks meant that he soon became 'linked' to literally dozens of women, often celebrities whom he had merely met at a premiere or party only once! It was a trickle at first, but soon it became almost a hobby to link Chace with any number of hot females – Lindsay Lohan, Taylor Momsen, Emma Roberts, Kim Kardashian for example (all denied). In interviews he would constantly be asked which celebs he found hot – some of his answers surprised a few people, such as saying he found Sarah Palin very attractive! Conversely, one fan told a reporter that she thought supermodel Cindy Crawford was his mom! More often than not this was all just mischievous reporting; for example, the 'date' with Kim Kardashian was a rumour that spread after the two had co-presented an award at a ceremony and apparently 'hit it off'. There was nothing more to it than that.

Perhaps predictably there was also talk of on-set romances, with Leighton Meester being 'linked' to Chace, something that was again denied by both parties. While denying any alleged romance she was happy to point out how good their friendship was: 'I'm really close to Chace. We're really good friends. [Along with] Nicole [Fiscella], who plays Isabel on the show. We're all just really happy people. We have the same views on life.' She went on to suggest that many of these rumours are the result of a blurring of the lines between fact and fiction: 'The biggest thing I've noticed is they kind of want everybody to be their character. Like Leighton [dating] Chace, and me and Blake hating each other. Those are our characters on the show – that's not us in real life.'

Chace muddied the waters himself though when he revealed some of his own techniques for getting close to a girl; given that he'd previously dismissed various rumours of relationships by saying a particular girl in question was 'just a friend', quotes such as the following only served to confuse! 'I try to get to know the girls I'm attracted to without having an official "date". I keep it light, become their best friend and hold off on the romance. If you're friends first, the rest of it happens more naturally.'

So what sort of girl would Chace like to date and how exactly would he go about it? Cooking seems to be the food of love. 'I love to cook,' he told MediaBlvd.com. 'I can make a mean spaghetti. I try to eat healthy – egg whites and all that.' He's also reported to be a dab hand at barbecues but also thinks if a girl brought a McDonald's to a date he'd be impressed! 'All you need is a pool table, beer, an electric jukebox and good conversation,' he once told *People*. One of the best dates he has been on was with a girl who wanted to go camping so they packed the car, drove to California and stayed for five days. Or perhaps he will find love on the golf course? 'It'd be nice to get old and have someone to play golf with.' He'd certainly be impressed if his date wanted to go to see his favourite teams the Dallas Mavericks or the Cowboys too!

Perhaps this gives a hint as to his long-standing love for Texan girls who obviously still hold a special place in his heart: 'Being around Texas girls all my life, that's what I'm used to. Maybe it's their charm, the way they're raised, their decorousness … and that's taught me a lot about what I'm gonna want from a girl eventually. I'm using a French phrase to describe a Texan girl but they have a … *je ne sais quoi*.'

Top tips on what to avoid on a first date are: 'an obnoxious laugh, swearing like a sailor, bad breath, breaking wind, getting blackout drunk, talking about your exes. It's a long list!' He thinks women worry too much about love handles, that there's too much pressure on them to be super-slim and he does think that everyone has 'a handful' of soulmates out there. For him, the single biggest draw would be a girl who makes him laugh. He has teasingly said he has 'experienced' love at first sight, but gives no further details.

He is certainly the romantic: 'Being romantic is subjective,' he told *Cosmo*. 'I think it's more about being creative; going outside the box. I don't do anything formal but I love to draw pictures for a girl, or take her to a concert. I don't do cheesy chat-up lines.'

Chatting up a girl now is riddled with complications too – Chace's fame has a downside in this respect in that he finds that he's not always certain about a girl's intentions when they meet. As a result, he is more cautious about new relationships.

He has even joked that he might be better off dating anonymously online. Given his massive internet fan base and the huge number of chat rooms and forums dedicated to Mr Crawford, one can only imagine the thrill this statement sent around the world of online Chace lovers!

Seriously though, this aspect of fame doesn't worry him because he is in no rush to settle down; he cherishes the idea of a loving wife and kids at some point in his life, but for now he is clearly enjoying his 'hottest bachelor' status, something that is not about to change. When he does finally get hitched, he wants two or three kids, a couple of dogs and a big house near a lake, but Chace fans might have to wait a while yet to pop the question: 'I don't trust myself to get married in my twenties,' he candidly told *People*. 'I don't feel like I'm mentally there yet; right now, I'm having more fun than most 23-year-olds should be allowed to have! I'm not in any rush.'

CHAPTER 8

Not Exactly The West Side

WHILE CHACE'S PERSONAL LIFE was being pored over by the media, so too was that of his character in *Gossip Girl*, as the show became ever more popular. In Season 3 the 'nearly there' love affair between Nate and Serena reignites, and yet our man Chace/Nate is still never quite able to get sorted! This time as the ill-fated pair are about to kiss (again) they are interrupted and Nate is left heartbroken once more, only for Serena to do exactly the same again shortly after ... two rejections for the price of one. By now Chace/Nate fans were painfully sympathetic to their hero's woes. In interviews, this sympathy is often visible in the way that journalists talk to Chace – friendly, kind, slightly patronising sometimes, whereas with Ed/Chuck they talk much more directly, and even with some caution! Still, in this third season Nate wins the day and eventually, in Episode 13, he and Serena finally become a couple! The cheer that went up around the world was almost audible when this finally happened. It's short-lived, however, and before the season finale Serena has broken it all off again. Scorned, Nate closes the season with two women on his arm. His fans were thinking: *Yes, but that's not what he really wants* …

What Chace Crawford really wanted in real life was to keep extending his movie career. His work rate showed no sign of letting up when he took a role in yet another movie, this time in the Joel Schumacher directed *Twelve*, based on the Nick McDonell novel of the same name (which the author wrote when he was just 17). A new street drug called Twelve – a drug said to be an instantly addictive cross between cocaine and ecstasy and favoured by socialites who would not be out of place in *Gossip Girl* – has led to the deaths of several people and the film follows the drug's path of destruction as it demolishes the lives of many people, some metaphorically and some literally. Chace's character is called White Mike, an impoverished Harvard student and son of a rich restaurant tycoon who postpones his university career to sell illicit drugs to his former classmates, so a somewhat different personality to the squeaky-clean and privileged Nate Archibald that he had become so well known for! (Some sources had Schumacher himself describing the film as '*Gossip Girl* on steroids'.)

Chace himself described White Mike as 'dark, serious and tragic', although it is worth noting that Mike himself does not use drugs or alcohol. In the film his character's mother had died one year previously and he was struggling to cope with the loss and his empty life, not least because her illness had financially ruined his family. His suppressed grief and sense of alienation from much of the world underpins large segments of the movie's plot and Chace's acting out of this painful sense of loss is acute and striking.

In this movie, Chace's character is the lead male, with much of the opening section of the film centering on him. Many of the key scenes in the movie revolve around or heavily involve his character – the murder of his cousin, various drug deals, a fateful confrontation with the drug Twelve's supplier (Lionel, played by 50 Cent), the climactic shoot-out at a party and the emotional closing scenes with his co-star Dionne Audain. Promotional posters would also feature Chace as the largest star, dwarfing the pictures of his co-stars such as 50 Cent and Emma Roberts.

Chace threw himself heartily into the major role, not just technically but physically too. Tabloid paps and even fans gossiped about how much weight Chace had lost – a physical transformation that was required for his drug dealer persona (some reports had the already lithe actor losing over a stone). He lived as a 'hermit' for weeks to strip the fat off him and also to take on the troubled persona of his character. Even his famously unblemished skin seemed to be pale and puffy, and he was often seen on set looking very scruffy and dishevelled – so much so that in between takes he found he could stroll around New York and no one even recognised him, quite a difference to the traffic jams he would cause when he was filming as Nate Archibald! He admitted he loved being incognito again. And the weight loss and less obvious 'pretty boy' looks reassured him that he could avoid that dreaded 'hunky' stereotype that he seems so sensitive to. That said, his character was still swirling around the Upper East Side of Manhattan's wealthy set, so in a sense there was a definite continuation from *Gossip Girl* too.

The whole atmosphere on set was also much more modest than the high-profile *Gossip Girl* circus. There was one trailer for the entire cast and a very strong sense of team spirit pervaded the whole shoot. This helped add to the dark intensity that Joel Schumacher was searching for. It was by no means all serious though – the cast often finished work and headed up to Chace's apartment where he has 'a world class roof-deck' and the party would start!

That dark intensity was helped enormously by some of the cast – most obviously 50 Cent who, as one of the biggest rap stars ever, was a huge bonus to the film's chances. Given Fiddy's own very traumatic childhood and his notorious gang experiences, some people wondered how he would get along with a southern boy who went to church and seemed to all intents and purposes to be his exact opposite. No such problems, in fact, there seemed to be a genuine affinity: 'The nice soap star, and the brutal gangsta rapper?' Chace pondered with *GQ Style*. 'Yes, yes. A supposition that it would be extremely close to potential conflict. Which of course it wasn't.

We got along just fine, I couldn't think of a better colleague. 50 Cent is a special person. And incredibly intelligent when it comes to career planning.' Chace clearly enjoyed working with the rapper and revealed a surprising soft side to the famously tough guy image: 'He's just a big jokester. [50 Cent] is like Mr Nice Guy Next Door. He gives everyone a big hug, makes sure everyone's having fun and keeps it light. I remember the day I was driving home from school and his first CD came on. I absolutely loved him, so [working with him] was pretty surreal.'

Another actor of note was the film's narrator, none other than Kiefer Sutherland who had made his own breakthrough in *The Lost Boys*, the film which Chace's first cinematic foray *Covenant* had been so poorly compared to, and which was the second so-called 'Brat Pack' film directed by Joel Schumacher (the first was *St Elmo's Fire*).

The film's director clearly made an impact on Chace; not surprisingly, perhaps, as Schumacher was one of Hollywood's most respected directors having been behind the lens for films such as those two Brat Pack movies but also blockbusters like *Batman Forever* and *Batman and Robin*, as well as successful but less commercial films such as *Flawless* and *Tigerland*. (Notably, Chace has said he would love to play the Caped Crusader in a movie adaptation and cites Val Kilmer as a key influence.)

Chace loved working with Joel Schumacher and in particular revelled in the artistic freedom that the director encouraged. Speaking to Christopher Bollen for *Interview* magazine, he said: 'It was much more of a low-key, smooth situation with Joel Schumacher running it. There were no big master scenes outside. It was more improv – just throw and go.' In the same interview he also said, 'I'm in awe of Joel. He's an artist. And he has such a vision that he makes you feel comfortable. Obviously, the role is a bit of a risk for me personally, but he gave me this confidence when he set a certain kind of tone or energy on the set. Joel's the man.'

Filmed in Chace's new home city of New York, the movie was a very edgy and fast-paced independent thriller, laced with credibility and certainly a very authentic progression in his big-screen career. The film was clearly being taken more seriously than *Loaded*, not least because its premiere was at none other than the critics' favourite Sundance Film Festival, on the last day of January 2010.

Critical reaction to Chace's new movie was mixed and box office takings were rather muted. In fact, some sources rate the box office as less than $200,000 in the first two weeks, with a global box office gross of around $2.5 million. In Hollywood terms this is not a large sum of money.

The depiction of violence and death was quite severe and some suggested that Chace's younger audience might find this upsetting, but it is ridiculous to expect him to restrict his roles to only those that satisfy the moral values of a very young fan base. This was inferred in a scathing review in the *New York Times* by Stephen Holden when he said that Chace had been 'painfully miscast'. His barbed pen wasn't reserved for just Chace, going on to say it was 'a tawdry melodrama' that was 'more interested in gaping salaciously at the depraved, joyless lives of the denizens [portrayed] ...'

Holden wasn't alone. Many critics felt the voice-over narration of Sutherland was superfluous and irritating; reviewers criticised the styling too, with the *Village Voice* saying, 'Though Crawford's bangs and facial hair are the most art-directed aspect of the movie, he's costumed to look like a member of the Trenchcoat Mafia.' *Rolling Stone* simply said it was 'a drag-ass slog'. In general, European critics reacted much more positively to Chace's part and the film itself, which suggested there might be a backlash against *Gossip Girl* in America that was colouring how people viewed Chace's latest efforts. Nonetheless, with comments like this from Wetpaint.com, it was hard to see how the new movie could benefit Chace's otherwise shining rise to fame: 'Chace Crawford (Nate) won't be winning any Oscars this year. The critics hate his new film *Twelve*. It's no shock the film was universally derided when it debuted at Sundance.'

So it was another sideways step at best in Chace's film career; however, although *Twelve* was neither a critical nor commercial hit, there was a sense that Chace was a natural on the big screen and there was a growing feeling in Hollywood that it is only a matter of time before he catches a role that will make him one of the world's biggest movie stars.

After the filming for *Twelve* had wrapped, Chace admitted that heading back to the frenzied circus that was shooting *Gossip Girl* had been something of a culture shock. 'I jumped back into *Gossip Girl* on a Monday,' he told Christopher Bollen, 'and I was so stressed the first day back. There's the first shoot of the episode on location, and it's triple the mayhem. Of course, it would die down in a couple weeks, but there were paparazzi guys flying around like wasps, completely disrespectful.'

Gossip Girl is famous for its so-called 'walk and talk' scenes, where key characters are filmed strolling along an apparently 'everyday' New York street usually having some emotionally drenched heart-to-heart. However, the reality is very different and Chace says this peculiar fact is one of the hardest and most challenging aspects of that show: 'You're walking and just talking about life and death,' he told Bollen, 'you're having a serious conversation, looking someone in the eye, but everywhere around you, it's literally a circus. Sometimes I sit back and laugh. But it definitely drains your focus and energy. I come out so mentally exhausted.' He compared the show's filming to going back to high school, in that you bump into all these people that you had been with the previous year!

By now another aspect of *Gossip Girl*'s appeal was almost as popular as Chace and his fellow actors! The fashion and style of the series has become a crucial part of its success and of course Nate and Chuck were instrumental in this. Chuck is clearly the most outrageous of the cast in terms of his clothing but Chace/Nate has developed a neat line in the most stunning designer suits and formal wear. Chace enjoys wearing the high-fashion tailored suits that Nate dons, and has increasingly been spotted in the front row of various catwalk shows, especially around Europe. Armani have in particular been very welcoming and although he claims he is no fashion or style icon as some observers would have it, he thoroughly enjoys this glamorous side of his job.

His own personal style has shifted too; notably in the pilot Nate's hair is gelled high but this was a look that did not return for the series run: 'I got them to comb it down, it was up in the pilot and wasn't me.' His floppy hair has since been mimicked by millions of boys and men around the world and even rivals that of vampirish Robert Pattinson. He tends to play down his style when asked about this in interviews: 'It's important to have a certain look in the industry but I honestly tend to wake up and comb my hair with my hands. I think I have three pairs of the same jeans, so when I find something I like, I tend to stick with it.'

Personally Chace likes more classical looks like Ralph Lauren and John Varvatos although he's also a fan of the more garish Dolce & Gabbana; 'I'm a friend of the subtle.' For a Texan native – an area that he has said is keen on the 'head-to-toe denim outfits', he certainly has some style. He told *GQ* that, 'I actually enjoy carrying a perfectly fitting suit. Because I just feel better in good clothes. Which I only know since I'm interested in cuts and styles.' Chace cites Paul Newman in *Cool*

Hand Luke as a style influence and also Steve McQueen. Notably, in real life Chace does not have a personal stylist, unlike many of his Hollywood peers, instead he chooses all his own clothing himself. He's also got heavily into luxury watches too, with premium brands such as Panerai, IWC and Audemars Piguet – which can cost five figures ... or even more.

The above reference to 'bangs' or a 'fringe' as it is known in the UK is a trademark look of Chace's, along with his eyebrows and those startling blue eyes. When he appeared on the front cover of *VMan* magazine, his gelled-back 1950s-style hair caused quite a few ruffled feathers among his online fan base who posted pictures of the cover within minutes of its release while chat rooms all debated if it was a good look or not!

Back on *Gossip Girl*, Nate's style was necessarily the subject of feverish debate among the producers and show's stylists. It was an important factual detail because any character in real life such as Nate would inevitably spend a massive amount on clothes. Nate's style has been described as 'casual chic'; the show's stylist Eric Daman is a master of his craft and his choices of clothing have contributed heavily to *Gossip Girl*'s success.

CHAPTER 9

Dark Times

With any big TV hit, there will always be criticism. It's impossible to please everybody and *Gossip Girl* was not immune to this problem. So by the end of the third season, with ratings up and the PR presence of the show and its lead actors and actresses never higher, there was something of a backlash against the glamorous programme. The criticism and controversy came on several levels.

Firstly, some observers criticised what they saw as an over-sexualisation of a show that was targeted at teenagers. The steamy sex scenes and relentless frolics were of course lapped up by the fans but this did not stop worried older minds expressing their concern. Writing in the *Independent*, Guy Adams gave a very balanced overview of the show and was very complimentary about Chace in particular, but did reserve judgement on some aspects of the programme:

'At the heart of the show, there lies an emptiness. Watching it can feel like scoffing fast food: it may serve a purpose, and will certainly tickle your taste buds, but you can't help worrying if it's all that healthy. Some of the show's fruitier scenes, many involving a half-naked Crawford, feel superfluous. And the storylines and values espoused by its sex-obsessed, often selfish and materialistic stars are what curmudgeons might call a sad reflection of the youth of today.'

Given the saucy nature of much of *Gossip Girl*'s storylines, Chace admitted that he was sometimes a little awkward about his family seeing the show. Having sex on a bar stool might not be what you want your mum to see, but he also revealed that his grandmother was an avid fan too, and would hold *Gossip Girl* parties with her elderly pals. On one occasion she phoned him up to chide him for the 'cougar' storyline when his character Nate went with an older woman. He joked that his granny and her friends 'represent all of the 65-and-over demograph' of the show round the entire world.

Other critics panned the 'predatory' lifestyles of the women and questioned the message this was sending out to the show's millions of female fans. Critics also derided the obviously materialistic focus of these people, the craving for possessions ahead of happiness. When some journalists called it 'a parent's worst nightmare', *Gossip Girl* – in a display of confidence in their show – simply turned this around and made it a slogan for a new set of adverts. Critics cried foul, saying they were not taking their influence seriously.

Chace admired this openness and said in the *Inquirer* that he understood some people's reservations: 'They [the show's creators] keep it edgy. That's part of the reason why our adult demographic is growing because there's a lot of adult material … [although] I wouldn't let a 13- or a 14-year-old watch the show.'

Chace himself came in for a fair amount of criticism too, sometimes exacerbated by the blurring of those lines between fact and fiction. Of course, Nate Archibald's privileged background made that character an easy target for snipers, but because Chace did not come to the table with stories of 'impoverished artist' in his portfolio, many detractors also said he'd had it too easy. He'd only been acting three years, they said, others suggested it was largely down to his good looks.

Chace had previously stated he knew the time would come when the almost universal acclaim would turn and he'd be criticised. He was ready for this and employed a sure-fire way to defuse this critical attack; his innate modesty: 'I realise how fortunate I am,' he told *Vman*. 'I had a lot of things fall into place, by chance, kind of a fluke. There was definitely a hint of good luck to it. But I do have a drive and a certain curiosity that not all people have.'

As a relative newcomer, he also finds the more pretentious side of Hollywood rather vacuous: 'There are a lot of people that try too hard to be the starving actor and to be really pseudo-intellectual and dark, when, really, there's a business side to manage and push towards.' And Chace leaves no stone unturned in proving his critics wrong – his ambitious drive is matched by a self-critical edge that means he always watches every episode at least once to check how he comes across and to spot any elements of his acting that can be improved. He finds watching himself on-screen uncomfortable but understands that this is one of the main ways he will improve.

Another problem *Gossip Girl* inevitably came up against was competition. The appeal of being the latest 'big thing' in TV-land is joyous but also by definition short-lived; for *Gossip Girl* there were soon rival shows vying for attention, such as *Criminal Minds* and *Grey's Anatomy* spin-off *Private Practice*. Some industry commentators suggested that for all the hype and massive online buzz about the show, the actual ratings were not quite as spectacular, with the first season notching up only 196th in the list of prime-time shows. Others said that the show had similarly modest ratings across the pond in the UK, so it could not be considered a truly international hit. Responding to this, Chace said, 'To be honest it's almost a blessing in disguise that it's not some massive mega *90210* that typecasts us and goes a decade. It's a bit more under the radar and cult in a way. I'm sort of fortunate for that.'

With so many good-looking and highly ambitious actors and actresses on set, it was also perhaps inevitable that rumours of catfights and squabbling started to surface. Speaking to the *Daily Goss*, Chace simply shrugged his shoulders and denied any such problems: 'That's the funny thing, they always try and twist our private lives. They want it to be like the show with the catfights but it's exactly the opposite. After an 80-hour week we'll be in the van exhausted and we're like, "Hey what you guys doing? Do you want to grab some food?" We're all very close and we're best friends. We get along very well, surprisingly I know. I wish it was more interesting.'

Unfortunately, the difficult times were not over yet because in June 2010 Chace made headlines once again and this time it was with regard to an incident in his personal life. Given Chace's very amiable persona and reputation within Hollywood for being a likeable guy with fierce ambition and drive, it was naturally with great shock that the world woke up on 4 June 2010 to reports of his arrest. He had been charged with misdemeanour and possession of marijuana.

According to reports he'd just returned from a lovely family trip to Mexico where he had spent the Memorial Day Weekend at a luxury resort with his sister Candice and her boyfriend, American football star Tony Romo (who had previously dated Carrie Underwood and Jessica Simpson). His parents were also on the trip.

Back in Plano, Texas, police said Crawford was sitting in a vehicle with a friend in a car park outside the Irish bar 'Ringo's Pub' just after midnight when he was arrested for one count of possession of less than two ounces of marijuana. Chace immediately insisted he was innocent and was simply in the wrong place at the wrong time; the worrying fact was that if convicted, court reporters suggested he could face up to six months in jail, or a $2,000 fine or both. Reports suggested it was one unlit joint that was found in the car and not on Chace himself. Chace was not smoking the joint at the time. 'Sources' adamantly denied the joint was his.

Soon after, both Chace's mug shot and the official police arrest documents were available to view online – listing his place of residence as New York. It was very shocking to see Chace's police photo spread across the Internet and it was not lost on the watching world that his character in *Gossip Girl* is a prolific pot smoker – again blurring the lines between fact and fiction.

Attention on the case was obviously high with one camera even turning up at the McKinney, Texas courthouse when he attended to listen to the formal charges. Chace was accompanied by two men – presumably security – and was wearing a white shirt and smart tie, but otherwise it was a very low-key court appearance. When the matter came to a resolution some time later, Chace agreed to perform 24 hours of community service, report to his probation officer every month and 'maintain good conduct' for 12 months. In return the case was dismissed and he would have no criminal record.

This came as a great relief to his millions of fans – in the past few years a large number of very famous and young stars had become embroiled in drug, drink and other scandals, so it was a relief that Chace was not to be one of these. Lindsay

Lohan is the most obvious example of an actor going off the rails with a litany of offences against her, along with spells in rehab and jail; Britney Spears is another female star who has battled scandal. Chace was not about to join any such list. Despite the negative headlines of the marijuana incident, Chace is actually a clean-living boy – although he once got two speeding tickets in one night, one when he picked up his girlfriend in his seventies Dodge Challenger and one when he'd just dropped her off!

In a strange and equally innocuous parallel to her brother, Chace's sister Candice was arrested in 2007 for alleged 'underage possession of alcohol' at a bar on Columbia, Missouri. With the spotlight on her as well as her brother, Candice's love life has become the source of media attention and interest too. Since 2009 she had dated the star quarterback of the Dallas Cowboys Tony Romo and in May 2011 they were married in front of 1,600 guests. Inevitably, comparisons are made in the media between the two well-known siblings, with perhaps the most superficial and comical being 'they have the same eyebrows'. The regional publication *D Magazine* named her one of 'The 10 Most Beautiful Women in Dallas 2010'; DFW.com named her one of the 11 'Hottest people in North Texas'. It's all in the jeans (sic).

After this small stutter, Chace's stellar career was free to keep on exploding. The 'arrest' episode had certainly not affected his popularity one jot – according to one website, 'mug shot or not, Crawford still managed to look hot'.

CHAPTER 10

He's Just Getting Started ...

SEASON 4 TELLS US that thanks to Chuck's 'Little Black Book' Nate has been very busy sleeping around with numerous one-night stands. Even here, with behaviour that is not very becoming, Chace fans could forgive him; he is, after all, suffering from a broken heart! Maybe it's his stunning looks, maybe his soft demeanour, maybe it's the confusion between Nate and Chace, but whatever Nate gets up to on-screen seems to have little affect on Chace's popularity! Despite recent difficulties with the marijuana arrest and the backlash against *Gossip Girl* in certain circles, there seems to be no sign of Chace's celebrity declining.

Maybe Chace will break his 'critics' duck in 2011 with the release of his next movie project, *Peace, Love and Misunderstanding*. The independent comedy-drama is being directed by the Academy Award-nominated Bruce Beresford, perhaps best known for being behind the lens of *Driving*

Miss Daisy (which scooped an Oscar in 1990). Starring alongside Chace will be *Grey's Anatomy* actor Jeffrey Dean Morgan and Hollywood legend Jane Fonda. The film centres around a lawyer and her two children who visit their hippy grandmother at Woodstock. Chace plays a character called Cole who is billed as 'a war-protesting butcher who catches the eye' of the lead female's daughter – reassuringly this character doesn't sound too much like Chace's usual parts! At the time of writing it is unclear how substantial that role is. Much of the filming was on location in New York's Hudson Valley and was described by the *Hollywood Reporter* as 'a multi-generational indie flick'. His admiration for actors such as Leonardo DiCaprio who star in big blockbusters as well as indie films was obviously a key motivator behind Chace's decision to take the role; time will tell if it was a good call.

At the time of writing, Chace is also scheduled to star in *Responsible Adults*, a romantic comedy set to feature Katie Holmes, the wife of Tom Cruise. The movie is written by Alex Schemmer and will be directed by Jon Poll (various *Austin Powers* movies, *The 40-Year-Old Virgin*, *Dinner for Schmucks* and *Meet the Fockers*). Rumours suggest Holmes' character is a 32-year-old mum who seduces the younger man played by Chace only to find out that they'd already met many years ago when she was his babysitter! Chace will play a 22-year-old called Baxter Wood with shooting scheduled to take place in Los Angeles in late 2011.

Chace has also done some voice-over work for three episodes of *Family Guy* after meeting the show's creator Seth McFarlane at a party. On one episode, his voice was used during 'The Former Life of Brian', a reference to the famous Monty Python movie. Chace's character appears as 'a stranger at a gym' and offers steroids to the main characters who are struggling with their fitness. He also appeared on episodes called 'Stew-roids' and 'Dial Meg for Murder'. 'That,' Chace told *ES* magazine, 'was more of a dream come true than many things ... I get a good kick out of it, it's funny.' (He's also a big fan of *The Office*.)

Chace has also provided the voice for the John Connor character in *Robot Chicken*, an American stop-motion animated TV series that has a huge cult following. The show is a non-stop onslaught of popular culture references and surreal comedy, so it was a refreshing diversion for Chace to be involved. This is not mere jesting though – the 2008 'Star Wards' episode was actually nominated for an Emmy! Like many other cartoon and animated shows in the US, there is a tradition of celebrity guest voice-overs; Macaulay Culkin, Jean-Claude Van Damme, Snoop Dogg and even George Lucas have all chipped in, so Chace was in good company. The three episodes he has appeared in are called 'Cannot Be Erased, So Sorry', 'Terminator' and 'Maximum Douche'.

Any book on Chace Crawford can't be complete without a look at the similarities – and differences! – between him and the character that made him famous, Nate Archibald. It's a question that Chace is repeatedly asked in interviews and picks up again on the public's fascination between what they see on a TV screen and what a celebrity is like in real life. Chace says he does share some characteristics in common with Nate, although very much more toned down. He has never been in a love triangle, although as we've previously seen he did once date his ex-girlfriend's best friend, albeit 'way after. And no one cared, I was a dork!' Talking to *CW Source*, he happily admitted that in Nate's personality there is 'a lot of me in there as far as the emotional stuff and the family stuff.'

'I'd like to think that I have more of a sense of humour,' Chace told the *Daily Mail*, 'and am less uptight than Nate. I also lack his passion for all things navy!' Generally Chace champions Nate but he can also see his character's limitations: 'My character always takes the right decision,' he told *Cosmo Spain*, 'which can be a bit boring, right? In life you have to take risks! Nate is this undecided character, he never stops fighting for what he thinks he believes in. So we aren't alike: I'm a less serious guy, I try to take things more lightly!'

Nonetheless, he feels that on the more serious matters he and Nate do share some traits: '[We] both have a certain moral conviction in life,' he told *TV Guide*. 'At 17 there is not much else to have on your plate except what college you're going to go to and what girl you're dating or want to date. I can relate to that pressure a bit because our private school was a bit of the same. Nate also wants out. He doesn't know exactly what he wants, but he knows what he doesn't want and I can relate to that.'

Chace is also on record as saying the pressure of high school social circles is definitely something he can relate to, but when talk turns to Nate's parental pressure and his overbearing father, Chace is quick to point out how fabulous his own dad is: 'I have never felt like I don't have any limits like Nate does. His father is trying to force him down a particular path in life, and he is now starting to question his family situation, his girlfriend and his future.'

And despite their differences, Chace clearly has a very affectionate place in his heart for the character that changed his life: 'He's knows girls are attracted to him and he knows how to turn on that Jerry Maguire charm ... he steps back and realises what's right and makes right decisions but sometimes he gets drawn in and ... takes advantage of it from time to time ... Essentially he's a good guy, he's got a good heart.'

And so what next for Chace Crawford? At the time of writing he's still single and enjoying dating. He is now seeing the considerable financial benefits of his massive success and this has turned his mind to a few childhood dreams that he can now afford to fulfil. For example, he's always had ambitions to get a pilot's licence. One of his favourite movies of all-time is *Top Gun*, the Tom Cruise film about the elite US airforce squadron that was partly responsible for Mr Cruise becoming the biggest actor in the world. Being a 'Top Gun' would be Chace's ultimate job and he still watches this film at least once a month! He has credited Tom Cruise with being a major influence on his acting career – apart from *Top Gun*, he has openly said that Nate Archibald is heavily influenced by the Cruise title role in *Jerry Maguire* about an egotistical sports agent tussling with his conscience (which was a huge smash hit movie for Tom when it was released in 1996).

Perhaps the reasoning behind this 'dream job' gives some indication of where Chace wants his career to go next, because it is always film stars that Chace cites as influences rather than TV actors. Equally it is acting for films that he seems to love most, as he explained to *BuddyTV*: 'I haven't done too many of either, but I really do like working on films more. There's more freedom. Television feels a little bit restrictive, so far as the dialogue, and there's really no improv. The scenes are a little bit shorter ... So, films are kind of where my head's at ... In the future. I love the show [*Gossip Girl*] though, hopefully that lasts.'

With such a versatile range – despite critics trying to pigeonhole him – Chace seems destined to keep his profile and success going strong, even long after *Gossip Girl* has finished. With Season 5 underway and his fame showing no signs of dwindling, it seems that in time we will look back and realise that for Chace Crawford fans, *Gossip Girl* was merely the start of something very big indeed!

PICTURE CREDITS

Now flip the book to read all about Ed!